Centra'

P9-EDA-653

Red woods

Antonio

Creek

## QUARTERDECKS AND SPANISH GRANTS

*concerning Captain John Clar, his United States Navy career after graduation from Spain's Naval Academy; his visit to Mexican California in 1836 and again at the Capture in 1842; the historic Gold Rush voyage of Barque Humboldt; his purchase of Oakland site; settlement at Clarville; the land surveyor, Translator and Keeper of the Old Archives.*

dicho terreno en garantía de los siete mil pesos restantes.

Mr. Clear se obliga a perseguir según las leyes de los Estados Unidos a los squatters que hoi en el rancho de Peralta con el objeto de espulsarlos y hacerlos dejar las posesiones que tienen en dicho rancho y si los squatters volvieren despues de haberlos espulsado Mr. Clear se obliga a ejecutar los proQuarterdecks sentencia que se obtenga de los tribunales respecto de dichos squatters

Mr. Clear se obliga a respetar los contratos de arriendo que Dn. Vicente Peralta tiene celebrado con Mr. Harper y Cook.

Mr. Clear se obliga a cumplir con todas las condiciones espresadas sin atender a si los titulos de Peralta sean declarados buenos o malos por la Comision que nombre el gobierno de los Estados Unidos y a hacer de mi parte cuanto sea posible para la validez de dichos titulos

La leña que Dn. Vicente Peralta necesita para su uso particular podra tomarla de la parte del terreno que no sea vendido sin costo ninguno

Contra Costa California Octubre trece de mil ochocientos cincuenta y uno.

Vicente Peralta
John Clear

Testigos presenciales
Mariano Urita
Evaristo E Garin

Sepase por esta escritura de venta que yo Vicente Peralta en consideracion de la suma de (10,000) diez mil pesos que me han pagado en dinero contado y a mi satisfaccion segun la adjunta contrata con John Clear he negociado vendido y traspasado al mencionado Clear una porcion de terreno llamado el "Encinal" descrito en dicho Contrato habiendo declarado Clear que el tiene una cuarta parte de la cual una tercera pertenece a B de la Barin una cuarta parte a J R Irving y otra cuarta parte a los s.s. John C Hays y John Caperton y la otra cuarta parte a Vicente Alvarado ...

# and Spanish Grants

## C. Raymond Clar

Glenwood Publishers, Post Office Box 194, Felton, California

ISBN      911760-08-3

Copyright © 1971 by C. Raymond Clar

Set in Intertype Century Schoolbook,
captions in News Gothic

Paper: Hi-Bulk Offset from Wausau Paper Mills

Designed and printed at
Big Trees Press, Felton, California

*This is the story of a man*
*and the times in which he lived.*
*It is a story which bridges two cultures*
*that were centuries apart.*
*One was proud, ancient, and decadent.*
*The other was proud*
*and sure of Destiny*
*with the arrogant assurance of youth.*
*The man was born in Imperial Spain*
*and he died in the fullness of time*
*at his home in San Francisco.*
*During that great human drama*
*which was the American occupation of California*
*he found himself standing*
*within the bright spotlight of history.*
*This is his story,*
*which in its telling*
*must include the story of others*
*who, with him,*
*loved and hoped and labored*
*and then quietly departed.*

U.S.S. Constellation

# Table of Contents

# List of Illustrations

# Introduction

It was not until early 1960 that I found it possible to seriously undertake the task of researching and writing a biographical sketch of the grandfather whose birth preceded my own by a full ninety years. Quite naturally, I had heard numerous small stories about his adventures. And in the course of the writing project some factual basis for most of the anecdotes was discovered. Yet I cannot help but conclude that the sons of John Clar were actually not intimately acquainted with the reserved gentleman scholar who was their father. As a matter of fact, only the fortunate recovery of an unusual quantity of heretofore unknown documentary source material has made it possible for this biographer to recreate something of the image of a man who was once so much alive.

What must now be recognized as a preliminary sketch was published by the *Pacific Historian* in four issues beginning in November of 1961. A few years later I began the collection of new source material for a proposed slight revision of the original work within one set of covers. In a short time the dimensions of newly discovered source data, and especially the revelation of new facets of the comprehensive story began to develop to proportions as amazing to the biographer as it has been valuable to the finished work.

In contemplating the broad project I have come to believe that any lasting value which may be attributed to this work will be due to the effort made to reflect the great and sometimes violent social and cultural changes which occurred in California during the approximate first half of the 19th Century. Therefore, this book pretends to be something more than merely a biographical sketch of one of the supporting actors in a fascinating historical drama. It should be measured in terms of its contribution to what might be termed the secondary echelon of authentic California history.

The eminent scholar, George P. Hammond, was asked to read and comment on the manuscript. We were especially grateful when he chose to compose the "Appreciation" which follows. Quite naturally it was largely inspired by the acquaintance with the Spanish land and culture he acquired during the three years he spent as a visiting professor at the University of Madrid. As the recent Director of Bancroft Library and Professor of History at the University of California, Dr. Hammond was also well equipped to contribute a number of valuable editorial comments regarding the manuscript. For these kindnesses the publisher and the author are sincerely thankful.

C.R.C.

---

# DON JUAN JOSEF CLAR

## An Appreciation

*This is the true story of a foreign immigrant who became a substantial citizen of the United States of America. There were millions of his kind. This child, christened Juan Josef Clar y Seguí at his baptism in 1813, was by virtue of natural gifts and the forces of historical circumstance destined to live an interesting and contributive life.*

*Minorca is a craggy, poor island, nestled in the northeast corner of the Mediterranean Sea, close to the neighboring island of Majorca (famous for its resort city of La Palma) and the mainland city of Barcelona. Much of its fame rests on its chief port, Mahón, Clar's birthplace, a deep-water harbor, the finest on Spain's eastern coast. Its significance as a port attracted the nations of the ancient world, from the Phoenicians, Greeks, and Romans down to modern times. Seized by the British in the War of the Spanish Sucession in 1708, they held it for nearly a century, until 1802, when it was finally ceded to Spain. During this time, the port had taken on something of a British air. Nearby, they had built the village of Georgetown, laid out in 1771 by a British engineer, where members of the British colony lived. With English sailors on shore leave, and with money to spend, life in the town was probably a bit lively—and not only gave the Spanish youth of the locality visions of what they would do when they grew up, but enabled them to learn the rudiments of another language. As Captain John D. Whidden wrote of his boyhood in* Ocean Life in the Old Sailing Ship Days *(Boston, 1914), "To go to sea, become a sailor, visit foreign lands, and in due time become the captain of a fine ship, this was the goal to be looked forward to, the great aim of our lives."*

*In such an environment, where sailors of all nations, and especially British, came for shore-leave, a cosmopolitan spirit developed. Some of the people spoke Castilian, others their native dialect of Catalan, or French, or English. It was a favorable opportunity for an ambitious youth like Clar to gain, very early in life, some knowledge of the outside world, and to become proficient in several languages.*

*Clar's ancestors had for generations followed the sea. Evidently, too, they had achieved some distinction, for the young man is refer-red to as* Don *Juan Clar. To be poor but of good family was nothing unusual. Most of the Spanish conquerors, from the time of Columbus, fitted into this category. The lure of a better life elsewhere continued to attract many of Spain's youth. That, clearly, became the pattern of Don Juan Clar's life, too.*

*At the age of 8 years, or about 1821, so Clar wrote later in life, he "was baptized in salt water and visited every port in the Mediterranean and spoke all of its dialects." Brief and tantalizing though this statement is, it reveals that as a boy he, like his ancestors, took to the sea, presumably as a cabin boy, a job that might lead to advancement and possibly to command of a ship some day. He spent about ten years in these travels, in which his use of various languages must have made him a great asset to his superiors.*

*The American flag was no stranger in the Mediterranean in Clar's youth. The new nation, the United States of America, demanded the freedom of the seas, like every sovereign power, and traded in Mediterranean waters. On the northern coast of Africa, it met with opposition from the Barbary states—Morocco, Algiers, Tunis, and Tripoli, who demanded tribute from them as well as from other foreign vessels. England, chief of the world's naval powers, had found it expedient to pay duty to these "pirates" rather than to fight. Skippers of American ships, however, refused to knuckle under to such piracy. This led to the so-called Tripolitan War in the early 1800's in which American warships won luster and distinction. During this time, American vessels must have found the port of Mahón as a fine place for shore leave, recreation, or business. On one of these occasions, Clar went aboard the United States Frigate* Constellation, *apparently in the summer of 1832 at Mahón, and entered the Naval Service of the United States. Though his specific appointment is clouded in some obscurity, he apparently was a captain's clerk, but soon was appointed Professor of Mathematics. As such he drilled the midshipmen in mathematics, astronomy, and Romance Languages. Thus he began his career in the United States Navy.*

*Following his fourteen years as a naval officer, Clar participated both as a technician and a party of personal interest in the complex and often bitter history of land acquisition in American California.*

*This story has been carefully researched and presented for the reader who is interested in the workaday world of the people and the things which constitute the true fabric of our national history.*

*George P. Hammond*
*University of California*
*Berkeley, California*

---

Vaughan, Photo.    18 Third Street.

John Clar

# 1  Baptised in Salt Water

*I*t was as an officer on an American ship of war that he first visited the Province of Alta California in 1836. And he first gazed upon the unpromising village of Yerba Buena in 1842 when it consisted of a dozen structures with about forty inhabitants. Undoubtedly, he would have been amused then at any suggestion that this was to be his home for 35 years of his life. When he died there in 1884, a quarter million people lived in the cosmopolitan City of San Francisco. Newspapers wrote of him then as "a pioneer of pioneers," a "useful actor departed," a warm and congenial friend who had passed away.

The child Juan Josef Clar was born at half past two on the afternoon of May 13, 1813, in the City of Mahón on Spain's Mediterranean Island of Minorca. Thus was the event precisely recorded next day at his baptism in the parish church. His father Lorenzo and his mother Clara Seguí were established as "legitimately married" citizens of Mahón. So, too, had been at least five generations of the child's ancestors, according to the ecclesiastical records of that ancient city.[1]

The Balearic Isles, of which Minorca is the most easterly, had been the crossroads of conquerors and sea merchants since Phoenician days. Minorca had been a British possession for a full century prior to 1802, and the City of Mahón continues to retain the appearance of an English city.

---

[1] The child's middle name, biblical Josef, was unused after he first arrived in the United States. He was named for the paternal grandfather (who was also godfather). Present at the baptism and recorded by family name were other grandparents ("all of Mahón"); Eulalia Cardona, wife of Juan Clar; Mateo Seguí and his wife Juana Orfila (godmother). U.S. records, for no known reason, show John born in 1812; baptismal record says, "mil ochocientos y trece."

The surname probably originated as Claro — "bright, clear." It rhymes with **are** and is generally mispronounced and misspelled. The telephone directory of Palma, Majorca, in 1968 contained more than 40 Clar listings. The earliest antecedent of child Juan found in church records of Mahón was one Jorge Clar who married Margarita Oliver about 1670. The San Francisco **Chronicle**, Jan. 15, 1898, printed a small article titled "Clar's Hope for Millions" in reference to a claim initiated by the writer's Uncle Frank for a Florida land estate of a missionary priest named Seguí, an alleged grand-uncle of claimant.

In his sea-bound, windswept homeland the boy Juan must have seen many American warships enter Port Mahón and he probably talked with American seamen. During the decade preceding his birth the young western nation had been heavily engaged in the Tripolitan War. And after the War of 1812 two United States squadrons were assigned to regular Mediterranean Sea duty for a period of almost a century.

The youth had been born into a seafaring family of many generations. Unfortunately, he left but few written records of that family and of his early life. On the other hand, there is ample evidence that this master of eight languages was never averse to spinning long yarns about his adventures. Consider, for example, this excerpt from his obituary printed in the San Francisco *Examiner* on April 28, 1884:

> Captain Clar was too modest a man to assume prominence in these later days as a leader of the giants of '49, but all his acquaintances recognized in him a man of masterly qualities and sterling worth. Personally he was of genial disposition and splendid conversational powers which, however, bore too much upon the many and varied scenes of a life of travel rather upon those incidents of early California days which in these later times would make history. There is scarcely a part of the world he had not visited and from every part he brought reminiscences worthy of a master hand to paint.

In his advanced years this man wrote a lengthy personal letter to an associate of 1849, one A. M. Kenady. It sketched very briefly some of the highlights of his life. The reason for the drafting of that strangely modest yet boastful letter was difficult to comprehend until there was inadvertantly discovered a second letter between two other people written at about the same time. That second letter indicates very surely that the Clar-Kenady letter was in fact the plea of an ill old man asking for political assistance to retain his modest government position. The circumstances of the two letters will be explained in the course of events. In the meantime, excerpts from the autobiographical sketch will be quoted where they are most meaningful in the story ahead.[2]

---

[2]Alexander M. Kenady was one of the passengers on the ship **Alexander von Humboldt** as described in the later story. When the letter was written on Sept. 16, 1883, Kenady was Secretary of the Association of Mexican War Veterans, presumably in Washington, D.C. The letter was published as an obituary in an unidentified newspaper. The original or author's handwritten copy is deposited with Society of California Pioneers in San Francisco.

The Kenady letter contains the following information about the early years:

> At the age of eight years I was baptised in salt water and visited every port in the Mediterranean and spoke all of its dialects.
>
> At an early date I passed my examinations with honors at the Royal Naval Academy of San Fernando, Spain, and was appointed Navigator of the Seas at the age of 18. Shortly afterward, in 1832, I entered the U.S. Naval Service, rated as linguist of modern tongues, and when the rank of professor of mathematics was created, I received my appointment as such, and continued in the Navy 14 years, made several cruises around the world and was in every foreign naval station . . .

The author of that rather poetic recollection of a colorful youth could count three score and ten birthdays of a busy life at the time he wrote the words. His memory and his reporting were essentially correct. Fortunately, however, several archival sources provide more precise facts in the particular case as well as some other fascinating bits of history.

---

Father Maynard Geiger, archivist and historian at Old Mission Santa Barbara, aided the writer in securing archival material at Santa Barbara and Mahón. He doubted that phrase "baptised in salt water" referred to any ritual of the time and place.

The highest reward the Patriot warrior can desire, is his country's approbation.

Thos. a/s C Jones
U. S. Navy

January 1847—

# 2  Ships of War

$\mathcal{D}$on Juan Clar was indeed graduated from the Royal Naval Academy of Spain. However, some question remains as to whether a student of common ancestry would have been accepted for training leading to a career in the Royal Navy of that time. His academic experience appears to have been aimed at qualifying civil maritime officers.

The young man's official certificate of graduation, dated May 10, 1831, was nevertheless royally elaborate. The hand script is so formal and flowery as to offer translation difficulties. In fact, the original certificate or diploma, as reproduced and translated on following pages, would lead one to assume that in the society of that time and place the rather overwhelming list of titles claimed by the highborn gentleman heading the institution was intended to impress potential employers even more than the qualifications of young graduates.

Among the United States ships of war in the Mediterranean during this period was the Baltimore-built *Constellation*. This ship was one of the original trio of frigates authorized by the Continental Congress. She was a little smaller than the *Constitution* and the *United States*. Yet in 1832 the noble *Constellation* was already a legend, bearing the scars of successful encounters with English, French and pirate fighting vessels across the wide seaways.

The fast sailing *Constellation* was launched in 1779 and commissioned the first warship of the infant nation. Fortunately, this ancient vessel has been preserved. On the 4th of July, 1961, *Constellation* was dedicated as a permanent National Monument and is now claimed to be the oldest vessel afloat.

This American frigate carried 36 guns and 340 men. She was 164 feet in length and displaced 1278 tons. After having had extensive repair in 1812 the trim clipper-hull vessel must have presented a beautiful sight under sail, especially when running before the wind with "a bone in her mouth."

There can be little doubt that the young Mahonese, with the certificate of Navigator of the Seas in hand, went aboard Frigate *Constellation* and requested regular employment.

# DON JOSÉ DE QUEVEDO

## CHIESA, GONZALES Y FERNANDEZ, CABALLERO GRAN CRUZ

de la Real y militar órden de San Hermenegildo, Teniente General de
la Real Armada, Comandante general del Departamento de Cádiz, Pre-
sidente de todas sus juntas, Juez privativo de la conservacion de montes,
y aumentos de Reales plantíos de la comprehension de él, &c. &c.

Por cuanto en D. Juan Clar
concurren la suficiencia y demas buenas circunstancias que pre-
vienen los Artículos 2.º y 3.º del Titulo 8.º de la ordenanza de ylla
tricular p.ª egercer la plaza de Tercer Piloto particular
en los buques mercantes de la Carrera de Europa, y segun lo
acreditado en el examen que acaba de sufrir y en las campañas
que ha practicado; he venido en nombrar al referido D. Juan
Clar por tal Tercer Piloto particular
de la citada carrera. En virtud de este Nombramiento, firma-
do de mi mano, sellado con el escudo de mis Armas y re-
frendado por el primer Ayudante Secretario de esta Capitanía
general, tomada que sea su razon en la Comandancia militar de Marina del tercio ó Provincia que corresponda, po-
drá el interesado egercer esta plaza, guardandosele los pri-
vilegios y exenciones que con arreglo a la misma ordenanza
deben gozar los de su clase. Dado en San Fernando á
diez de Mayo de mil ochocientos treinta y uno.

El Com.te General int.

Nombramiento de Tercer Piloto particular
de la Carrera de Europa p.ª D. Juan Clar

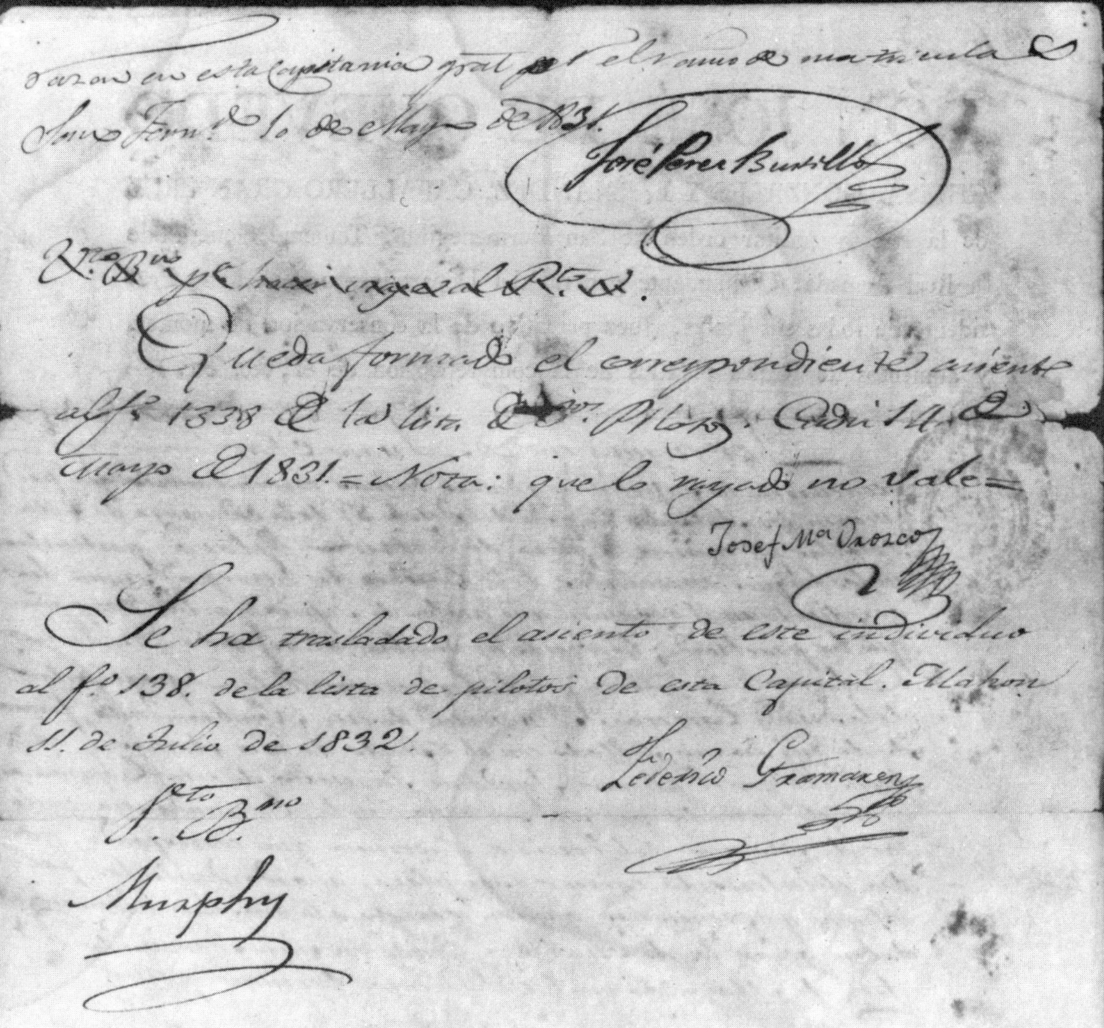

*[Handwritten cursive Spanish text, partially legible:]*

...en esta capitanía gral ... el ramo de matricula ...
S[a]n Fern[an]do 10 de Mayo de 1831.

*José Perez Bustillo*

...

Queda formad[o] el correspondiente asiento
al f[oli]o 1338 ... Pilotos. Cádiz 18 de
Mayo de 1831. = Nota: que lo rayado no vale =

*Josef M[aría] Orozco*

Se ha trasladado el asiento de este individuo
al f[oli]o 138 de la lista de pilotos de esta Capital. Mahon
11 de Julio de 1832.

*Lorenzo Garmaneny*

S[on]to B[uen]o

*Murphy*

Translation:
DON JOSE DE QUEVEDO CHIESA, GONZALES Y FERNANDEZ, KNIGHT OF THE GREAT CROSS of the Royal and Military order of San Hermenegildo, Lieutenant General of the Royal Navy, Commander General of the Department of Cádiz, President of all its Councils, Jurist responsible for forestry conservation and of all the Royal plantations therein, etc.

In as much as, in the person of Don Juan Clar are met sufficient and favorable circumstances as required in Articles 2 & 3 of the 8th. Paragraph of the qualifications to practice the duties of third class private pilot on merchant ships that ply European waters, as he has shown in the examination which he has recently taken, and as demonstrated in his practical experience. I therefore, name the aforesaid Don Juan Clar, Third Class Pilot, private, to practice in European waters. In virtue of this commission which I sign with my own hand, and to which I affix my own coat of arms, witnessed by the First Adjutant Secretary of this Captaincy General at the corresponding military Headquarters, the aforementioned individual may practice this profession, and is due all respect and privileges corresponding to those of his rank. Given in San Fernando the 10th. of May of 1831.

O. K. endorsements on reverse.
Note last one — "Murphy."

— Society of California Pioneers

The reverse side of the naval academy certificate was obviously used to indicate where the holder had registered with captains of ports. Presumably this established his qualifications as well as his availability for hire. The last such entry was made at Port Mahón on July 11, 1832. It seems logical to assume, therefore, that here in the city of his birth, the 19 year old Spanish youth "entered the U. S. Naval Service."

Two documents in Naval Archives make it amply clear that he signed aboard this American vessel, but there is a little confusion as to his official title. The rank of Professor of Mathematics had actually been in existence for a short time. However, it does not seem likely that a foreign youngster in a foreign port could have walked aboard a frigate and been promptly commissioned to such a rank. He seems to have been paid as a captain's clerk, and later appeared on a ship's roster under that title. Stronger evidence indicates that he enjoyed the unusual title of School Master.

In 1845 Professor Clar had reason to correspond with Secretary of the Navy George Bancroft. In that letter he recounted the highlights of his naval career. The first item is precisely quoted as follows, including the common spelling of cruise—" a cruize in the Mediterranean in the Frigate Constellation in the years 1832-33 & 34 as School Master. . . ."

Another valuable record is an undated payroll account of Frigate *Constellation* which seems to have covered all of the years 1831 through 1834. The various ratings, their date of signing on, and the rate of pay and deductions is set forth there.

For the period December 1, 1832, through December 13, 1834, one John J. Clar was listed on the *Constellation* roster with the title School Master. Aside from verification of the rank, the name of record is of interest. This is the only case of his middle initial having been used. More important, this young Spaniard demonstrated his clear intention of becoming an American. Now and henceforth he called himself John rather than Juan.

It would seem that citizenship was of no great importance among the crew, and possibly for officers, on an American warship at that time. The rough days of crew impressment were not long gone, and the cat-o-nine-tails colored one man's back as bloody as the next. A number of Spanish names were entered on the ship's roster of *Constellation* among new crew members. Probably this was a reflection of the normal crew attrition on all ships of that period due to death and desertion.

The payroll of the frigate reveals the salary of a lieutenant as having been 50 dollars monthly, plus a ration allowance. Midshipmen received 19 dollars and rations. Seamen, craftsmen and other crew ratings messed on galley food. Seamen received 10 or 12 dollars and a Ship's Boy, 1st class, received eight dollars a month.

School Master Clar was clearly a junior officer, with monthly pay of 25 dollars plus a 15 dollar ration allowance. The young teacher probably approached with utmost seriousness the task of drilling the midshipmen in mathematics, navigation, astronomy and the Romance languages. Without doubt he was at the same time making himself proficient in the use of the English language.

There was no American naval academy at this time. Youths of 14 or 15 years of age who hoped to become officers went to sea and stayed there. They endured a rough training for a strenuous career. Even younger lads signed on as ship's Boys. A rough and strenuous life was the life of a sailor in wooden ships of war.

A dread scourge of smallpox descended over Europe in 1834 and *Constellation* was ordered back to the United States. Andrew Jackson was President. Relations with foreign countries were relatively calm. The youthful and expanding group of states extended to the Mississippi River, and the new nation was suffering turbulent growing pains. The slavery issue was already flaring up emotionally and politically. Texas and California as well as the Oregon country were no doubt prominent in the thoughts if not in the public comments of many active American expansionists.

Although the United States was not at war, the world was a troubled place. In the vast Pacific theater, England and France were testing the strength of weak governments and laying claim of sovereignty over ocean islands. Aggressive merchants were probably shaping national destiny as certainly as were government officials. Similar ambitions were quite obviously being gestated within the United States. Yet the scope of sovereign designs on the part of this nation seems to have been limited essentially to its present continental bounds.

All of the recently separated American Spanish colonies and those currently in revolt were very delicate areas, politically and militarily, for those persons who claimed American citizenship. Not only was there the hazard of becoming caught in a crossfire between Spain and the area in dispute; there were equally vicious disputes arising between some of the dismembered sections of dying New Spain.

Official policy and national interests kept the American Navy roaming the oceans. Although it was small and poor, the Navy had to be spread thinly around the world. Naval officers had to demonstrate strength and determination at certain times and places, and always with a reciprocal friendship among friendly peoples.

The cost of maintaining a wind-driven warship was less at sea than at dockside; and the cost of maintaining a sloop was less than half that of a frigate. And that, no doubt, accounts for the fact that a sloop often served as a flagship for the highest ranking sea-going officer, the commodore. Technically, of course, a commodore was supposed to exercise command over the movements and activities of several war vessels in consort. The officer in command of his flagship, of whatever rank, was always referred to as the captain.

Commodores on long voyages were clothed with unusual authority as representatives of their nation in all the far places of the world. Sometimes a period of a half year or more would elapse without a direct exchange of messages between them and their homeland superiors.

It was inevitable during such lengthy voyages that seamen would occasionally desert their ships in a foreign port. Some men died from sickness or injury and found their final resting place in the deep sea or in the soil of some alien land.

———————

The first United States war vessel to sail along the shore of Upper California appears to have been the Sloop *Ontario*, Captain James Biddle. In August, 1818, this little ship touched at Cape Disappointment where Biddle nailed a lead plate to a tree claiming the Oregon Country on behalf of the United States. This was, of course, an obvious but quite ineffectual attempt to bar settlement by the Hudson's Bay Company.

On its homeward voyage *Ontario* tarried briefly at Spanish Monterey. It is doubtful if any official welcome was warmly extended. Spain in America was beset by troubles and foreigners were never welcome in the colonies. Revolutions of independence had begun to convulse New Spain. California was unconcerned and basically conservative. Because of this indifference the Argentine revolutionary Bouchard sacked and burned the tiny capital of Monterey in November of 1818, a few weeks following the visit of U.S.S. *Ontario*.

The next American warship to call at a California seaport was also a small sloop, named *Peacock*. This occurred in October of 1836.

The sloop *Peacock* had been circumnavigating the world during most of 1832, '33 and '34 when School Master Clar had been aboard *Constellation*. Its primary mission had been to transport the President's Special Diplomatic Agent, Edmund Roberts, while that gentleman negotiated trade agreements on the far side of the world.

Early in 1835 *Peacock* was outfitted and provisioned to repeat the long voyage with Mr. Roberts. The ship's company totaled 201 officers and men. Essential provisions for a three year voyage were stowed aboard. The Special Agent was prepared to deliver duly ratified treaties of amity and commerce to His Highness the Sultan of Muscat in Arabia and to his Magnificent Majesty, the King of Siam.

The sloop was to carry the broad blue pennant of Commodore Edmund P. Kennedy, Commandant of United States Naval Forces of the East India and Asiatic Station. Commander Cornelius K. Stribling was captain. School Master Clar, 21 years of age, was ordered aboard. The roster listed him as captain's clerk. Unquestionably, he was assigned to act as Commodore Kennedy's private clerk during the voyage.

Fleet Surgeon William Ruschenberger wrote a valuable narrative account of the voyage which extended into the years 1835, 1836, and 1837. He described the *Peacock* as being 118 feet in length and 559 tons burden. This ship had been completely rebuilt in 1828 with improved hull lines. Later it was discovered that too much heavy armament interfered with her sailing qualities and stability. In 1835 the doctor wrote:

> She has a light spar deck which frees the guns from the encumbrance of rigging. . . . In other respects the ship has no commendable quality. She is an indifferent sailer, very wet, and, for both officers and crew, the accommodations are very limited. She is armed with twenty 31-pound carronades and two long 12-pounders.[3]

Presumably the 12-pounder cannon could be moved fore and aft as desired. The spar deck extended in from the ship's rail over the guns on the main deck below.

---

[3] W.S.W. Ruschenberger, ship's surgeon on **Peacock**, wrote the 560 page book, **A Voyage Round the World.** (Phila. 1838). Few names other than principals are mentioned. Details of voyage and national goals are well told.

As a consort vessel the 10 gun Schooner *Enterprise*, Lieutenant A. S. Campbell, went along. This vessel made such slow progress that the Commodore ordered the respective captains to meet at determined rendezvous points rather than try to sail together.

At sunrise on April 23, 1835, in New York Harbor, the order was given by the boatswain of Sloop *Peacock*, "All hands, up anchor." They were under way, bearing south through the rainy spring months.

By June 10th the little squadron had raised the coast of Brazil off Río de Janeiro. Here the *Peacock* approached the United States Sloop *Natchez* and hove to. Both vessels fired 13 gun salutes. Then the *Peacock* substituted a red commodore's pennant for the blue in honor of ranking Commodore James Renshaw who was aboard the *Natchez*.

In early July, *Peacock* and *Enterprise* departed from Río and rounded the Cape of Good Hope. They cruised through the Mozambique Channel with no unusual event and made a call at Zanzibar.

At Zanzibar these representatives of a western nation which was itself heavily involved in a slave labor economy were clearly not cheered by the sight of public slave markets. They learned that about two-thirds of the local population were working in bondage.

The ships weighed anchor at Zanzibar on the 8th of September. And before two weeks had passed the officers and men of Sloop *Peacock* were trying to cheer each other with very grim jokes of what they expected to be doing as slaves of the Oman Arabs. That possibility had been very real and it came about in the following manner.

Sloop *Peacock* bore north northeast from Zanzibar about sixty miles off the coast of Africa. The little vessel was quite alone on the green Indian Ocean. Weather was fresh and brilliant. At night the sailors watched the changing phosphorescent display in the marine world below them. They crossed the equator and then passed beyond the wide mouth of the Gulf of Aden which is the outlet of the Red Sea.

On the evening of September 20 all was well. Studding sails were set alow and aloft. *Peacock* was logging a comfortable seven or eight knots. A sounding at sunset found no bottom with the hundred fathom line. All was secure, and only the watch on deck remained awake. Then at 2:20 a.m. "all hands were roused from sleep by a horrid noise caused by the ship's bottom grinding and tearing and leaping on a bed of coral rocks."

The helmsman quickly came hard over to starboard to lose the wind. Fortunately, the hull was not crushed on the first impact. Yet the sloop was soon fast aground. There was promptly much action but little confusion aboard. Sails and spars were brought down. Five thousand gallons of water were pumped overboard to lighten the burden. This forfeiture became a serious matter later when a hard laboring crew required extra water rations.

Dawn revealed a raw desert land some three miles to the east. Eventually it was determined that this must be the south end of the Island of Mazeira (Moseirah, Al Masirah) some 250 miles south of Muscat. They had been certain that the ship had been far to the eastward. The navigators naturally suspected chronometers and poor charts. Later an East India Company official told of English vessels running aground in this vicinity because of a chart error, but principally because of strong ocean currents.

A raft was built to support spars, working gear and provisions. Cannon balls were heaved overboard. At 10 o'clock a canoe with four Bedouins approached. Captain Stribling sent a small boat to communicate. In response the wild and half-naked visitors did little but threaten and wave their swords. Some of their brethren on the island shore appeared equally inhospitable.

The *Peacock* small boats found that the sloop would have to be moved 300 yards south to again float in free water. Ketch anchors were set in that direction and lines brought taut by the capstan spool. One anchor fluke broke; chain hawser lines were lost. The *Peacock* was fast aground.

Four Arab dhows approached and began to circle the American ship. In addition to the Negro oarsmen, who were undoubtedly slaves, there were 29 fighting men aboard the pirate ships. They were armed with spears, swords and old matchlock guns.

Eventually a canoe with an old graybeard and a handsome dark companion ventured near the warship. Sign language and gibberish apparently convinced them that their throats would not be cut if they came aboard the sloop. This they did. The pair strode the quarterdeck quite nonchalantly through groups of silent American sailors and marines. The latter were significantly employed at sharpening pikes and cutlasses.

Commodore Kennedy, Captain Stribling and, no doubt, clerk and interpreter John Clar listened to the palaver of the old man as the two visitors munched on sea biscuit and sugar. Not much was understood except that for one thousand dollars a message would be taken from the Americans to the Sultan of Muscat.

It is probable that all parties to this colorful conference understood that the pirates were interested solely in observing the strength of their intended victims. This accomplished, the Bedouins walked to the rail and jumped gracefully overboard, dressed as they were in large turbans, loose pantaloons with naked sword stuck in the waist sash. They recovered their canoe and paddled back to their companions.

Water rose about a foot an hour in the bilge, which in itself was not highly alarming. Passing of time caused most concern. The crew was showing signs of extreme fatigue. Weather was fair but hot. Half the heavy guns were heaved overboard on Tuesday, September 22nd. If the hull careened at low tide it would be impossible to bring the large guns into action, so spars were used as props between hull and coral rocks.

Before daylight on this Tuesday morning a course of action was considered and undertaken. It was hazardous, but so was the situation for the entire party. Midshipman Taylor and six selected men were ordered to try for Muscat in the sloop's cutter. Mr. Roberts, who no doubt viewed the delivery of the treaty papers to the Sultan as the all-important mission, volunteered to go.

Passed Midshipman William Rogers Taylor, with his first serious command, stood seaward. Looking to the northwest, this small company in a 26-foot sailboat observed with no little surprise that the *Peacock* was aground on the shallows of what must be Mazeira Island.

For five hours a pirate dhow gave chase to the small American boat. Then darkness and heavy seas permitted the latter to escape. Five days later, on the morning of Saturday, the 26th, Mr. Taylor brought his cutter and all hands safe into Muscat harbor.

Back at the stranded *Peacock* the desperate work went on. More Bedouin pirates surrounded the sloop and its small boats. They tried especially to steal the raft. Occasional cannon shots kept them at a respectable distance. Then on Thursday morning the *Peacock* was dragged off the coral ridges by capstan and kedge lines. For 56 hours her keel and coppered hull had been grinding on the rocks.

Without delay spars were raised and sails set for the northeast. After two days sailing the American vessel met an Arab sloop of war off the eastern tip of Arabia, Cape Ras al Had. Midshipman Taylor was aboard.

His Highness Syed Syeed bin Sultan had demonstrated both his great friendship for the Americans and the power of an absolute monarch. Immediately upon his being informed of the plight of the *Peacock*, three hundred and fifty Beduoin cavalrymen were sent galloping south along the coast of Arabia to inform the various tribal sheiks that if any American came ashore and was harmed the shieks would be considered responsible and lose their heads. Four war dhows with 300 men, under command of a provincial governor, were dispatched south to scatter pirates, to aid Sloop *Peacock*, and to recover lost or looted property.

On September 29 the *Peacock* sailed into the granite walled harbor of Muscat which has sometimes been called the hottest city in the world. Friendly Arabs smiled when the Americans complained of the fall temperature standing a little above 90 degrees. On the 5th of October Sultan Syed was a guest on board the American warship. With the mutual treaty happily delivered and acknowledged the *Peacock* on the 10th departed for Bombay, primarily to take advantage of East India Company drydock facilities there.

By early November the Sultan of Muscat had seen to the recovery of eleven *Peacock* heavy guns and some broken spars. These he shipped to Bombay while the refitting and bottom work was in process.

Schooner *Enterprise* arrived at Bombay and the officers and men of both American warships saw many wondrous sights during their 42 days ashore. But they departed Hindoostan with no great regrets. Some British residents were clearly suspicious and displeased in respect to the friendly association known to exist between the American Government and the Sultan of Muscat.

In early December the increasing deterioration of health of the entire command began to appear serious. No doubt they were suffering from malaria. When the *Peacock* arrived at Bombay the ship's surgeon had considered the numerous mosquitos to be a nuisance worthy of an incidental comment in the record. But in reporting later upon the common fever, he seemed to be certain, as had his predecessors for centuries before him, that the illness was "brought on by exposure, during their night watches, to the night winds which came to us loaded with miasmata, exhaled from the marshy land over which they blew."

Fortunately, the wind out on blue sea water seemed to greatly improve the general health of the men before the two vessels entered Port of Columbo, Ceylon, on December 15th. Because these were the first United States warships to visit this place, flagship *Peacock* saluted the harbor fort with 21 guns. The honor was returned in kind.

The ships left Columbo and sailed southeast to meet the new year at the equator. On January 10, 1836, the green mountains of Sumatra were sighted through black masses of monsoon clouds. On the 13th, the ships arrived in the seaport of Batavia (Jakarta), Java. All hands had been hoping that the first mail from home would be awaiting them here. They were disappointed.

Continuous heavy monsoon rains and a wild, dangerous sea kept the American ships in Batavia Road much longer than they had wished to stay in this unhealthy, politically unhappy Dutch colonial seaport.

On February 16th the vessels started moving north through the Java Sea. Before they had progressed far, two *Peacock* men were buried at sea; the first deaths of this voyage. The dreaded scourge of land armies and sea travelers, dysentery, had come upon them.

The ships coasted north between the Island of Bangka and Sumatra and thence along the east coast of the Malay Peninsula. By March 24th the Americans were at the mouth of the Mother of Rivers whereon stood Bangkok and the palace of the Lord of the White Elephants, His Magnificent Majesty, the King of Siam.

A great bramble of etiquette and protocol delayed the meeting of Mr. Roberts and the King until April 18. Then the mutual treaty was duly accepted and acknowledged, but not without quibbling. By that date cholera had appeared on board the *Peacock*. The commodore became ill, but not seriously. A seaman and a marine died, probably from cholera. Fortunately again, when the ships put to sea, the disease subsided. Yet near the Island of Poulo Obi, at the southern tip of Viet Nam Peninsula, another marine lad was buried at sea.

For a month along the coast of Cochin-China (Anam; Viet Nam) the Americans tried to find some responsible authorities, or to reach the Emperor at Hué, to discuss trading arrangements. Mr. Roberts had tried to lay the groundwork for treaties in 1833. Now he was ill and unable to play diplomatic games with disinterested officials. It would appear that some French influence within the mysterious oriental government maze was doing the United States trading ambitions no service in Cochin-China in the 1830's.

On May 21, Schooner *Enterprise* arrived at Hué with most of her crew seriously ill. Both ships departed into the Gulf of Tonkin in the evening of the following day. On the 24th, the ships sailed past Hainan Island in fair weather as the ship's band on *Enterprise* played "Home, Sweet Home." There was great hope for mail from home and better health at Macao.

On May 26 they anchored off Macao and began arranging to move the sick to shore with the help of American missionary doctors and British colonial medical and hospital staff.

Macao was ostensibly a Portuguese possession. But of 25,000 population only some 4,800 were Portuguese. And of these, the amazing statistics reveal that about 1,300 were white Portuguese slaves.

On June 5, 1836, death came to Lieutenant Archibald S. Campbell, Commander of the U.S. Schooner *Enterprise*, "an amiable and worthy gentleman." The officers and men of both ships erected a monument over his grave in the British cemetery.

On June 12, 1836, died Special Diplomatic Agent Edmund Roberts, Esquire, a native of Portsmouth, New Hampshire. To mark his resting place at Macao a monument was established by the concessionaire American Merchants Resident in China.

Promptly upon the arrival of the two United States warships the Chinese authorities began to press them to depart. It was doubted that contrary winds had forced them to come here as the respective captains had declared. War junks were anchored around the American vessels and the shore movements of all personnel reported upon. Their loitering, it was said, might give rise to *business*.

American Consul Snow, when directed to "hasten, hasten" the departure of the ships, was also furnished a Chinese inventory of each vessel's armament. He was assured that "Sze-kin-lun" (Peacock) had three masts, 190 sailors, 22 great guns, 100 muskets, 100 two-edged swords, 800 catties of powder and 800 cannon balls. He was also advised that *Peacock* possessed another set of side gun ports not mounted.

Some of the Americans, nevertheless, travelled by ferry some 60 miles up the Pearl River to the foreign trading concessions at Canton. And the sick men improved enough for both warships to weigh anchor with their remaining complement of men on the afternoon of June 23, 1836.

In a few days they passed close by the southern end of Formosa. The health of the men began to improve noticeably. On the 14th of July they anchored in the sparsely settled port of one of the Bonin Islands group, south of the great forbidden Island of Japan. They tarried there a week.

Sometime earlier, Purser J. D. Mendenhall had been moved from the *Enterprise* to the flagship with the hope that the best possible care would cure the illness he had contracted at Bangkok. However, the much respected officer died, and as the sun crossed the meridian on July 25 his coffin was slid into the blue sea with solemn ceremony. Saddened officers and men of both vessels stood at attention while the Christian burial service was recited and a ship's bell tolled his requiem.

The warships labored eastward along the northern edge of the tropics. Weather was generally invigorating, and the remaining sick men became stronger. Morning sunshine greeted the helmsmen through the forward rigging. On many afternoons great cloud mountains piled up at the edge of the stretching blue sea beyond the little vessels.

During a foggy night in early August the ships lost contact. Each pursued its separate lonely way. On the 10th day of that month Sloop *Peacock* crossed the International Date Line. There was some feeling of turning homeward among the men. They had been on the journey nearly a year and four months now.

On the afternoon of September 7th *Peacock* was within the Sandwich Island group. At sunset she dropped anchor off Honolulu which was the capital city of the King of Hawaii. The *Enterprise* had arrived the day before. Several days after the arrival of the little American squadron, King Kauikeaouli and his court received the officers. An American missionary translated the Polynesian dialect for them.

Commodore Kennedy conducted several local affairs of state with the king on the basis of a treaty created a decade earlier by the monarch and the then American Navy Captain, Thomas ap Catesby Jones. Captain Stribling, on his part, transmitted a "brotherly" letter to the royal lady, "Kinau, High Chief of Oahu." His advice for the improvement of local government and social development could be regarded as patronizing interference from a foreign official. On the other hand, there is no reason to suppose it was anything other than good will on the part of the American Government toward a small, independent, and helpless native kingdom at the cross-roads of Pacific commerce. Some representatives of England at this time were attempting to lay claim to the islands as a British possession.

On September 26th the *Enterprise* was instructed to sail east with two merchant vessels bound for Mazatlán. On October 9, the *Peacock* weighed anchor in Honolulu harbor and set sail northeast for Alta California. However, before the American ships sailed away from Hawaii, the Commodore received a letter compiled by 29 "undersigned citizens of the United States of America, resident at the Sandwich Islands." They were, they said, interested in "commercial operations conducted from the United States, China, and these Islands, to the coasts of California and Mexico."

The merchants complained in general about "serious outrages and unjust acts committed by the governmental authorities of those countries upon American vessels and seamen, and great losses sustained." Specifically, they pointed out injuries done to the well-known sea captains Gorham H. Nye and Alpheus B. Thompson, as well as ship owner John Coffin Jones, currently United States Consul in the Sandwich Islands. None of these three had, incidentally, signed the letter.

The plaintiffs stated in part:

> We believe that no vessel of the United States government has, for many years, visited Upper California; and we have great confidence that were a naval force to appear on the coast . . . it would render valuable service to our citizens residing in those countries, and would afford needed succor and protection to American vessels . . . with result peculiarly advantageous to our national commerce . . .
>
> With due considerations of respect
> We remain, sir, your fellow citizens.

It is interesting to note that the fleet surgeon of Sloop *Peacock*, in his narrative report of this event, was observant enough to comment upon the failure of his government in not providing an American consul for the Sandwich Islands with an adequate salary and the insistence that he not be personally involved in commerical affairs. It seems that the popular Mr. Jones was engaged in other regions on such personal business at this very time.

American resident merchants and sea traders dominated the commerce of Alta California. Officially, the Mexican Government was continuing the original Spanish disapproval of excessive contact with foreign nationals. Undoubtedly, the majority of the *rancheros* were anxious to acquire modern commodity goods, offered at high prices, in return for their rawhides and beef tallow. But they were at the same time unhappily aware of the growing influence of the increasing immigration of *Anglos* into California.

Import duties were a very important source of support for the government of this outpost province of the unsettled Mexican Nation. And the avoidance of such duties, through bribery and smuggling, was a well-known fact. Had they been asked, the responsible officials of Alta California, in the fall of 1836, could have presented a substantial bill of particulars in complaint against foreign, and especially United States, traders and ship masters in respect to dubious political and business behavior. In fact, Commodore Kennedy was soon to receive some advice in that respect.

In addition to this essentially local situation, there were broader international implications bearing upon Alta California. Russia, France and England were very much interested in the fate of this promising land. British commercial interests were appealing to their government to simply take California as repayment for some 50 million dollars owed England by the Mexican Government. And in some English minds the original claim to California (New Albion) by Sir Francis Drake was still valid. In 1835 the United States' interest had been shown by its tentative proposal to purchase the upper half of present California.

The log of Sloop *Peacock* for October 24-25, 1836, notes in part: "... at daylight discovered land on the lee bow bearing E.N.E. and E'ly. . . . moderate breezes and pleasant at 9 set the Mizen Top Gall't sail—Spanker, Royals & Flying Gib—got up and bent the Cables and got the Anchors off the bows."

And at noon of the 25th the log-day entry began: "Commences with moderate breezes and fair weather . . . at 1:30 gave Chas. Smith (Sea) 1 dozen with the Cats for disobedience of orders and disrated & reduced to the ranks George Holland-Master at Arms for playing cards and allowing improper lights on the Berth Deck.

At 4:10 called all hands bring ship to anchor, took in all sails and came in the Harbour of Monterey in 10 fs. water and furled sails . . . At meridian saluted the authorities with 21 guns which was returned by an equal number from the Fort."

Four merchant ships and two whalers were in Monterey harbor. They all flew the United States flag. A low morning temperature of 49 degrees was a little shocking but pleasant to the men of the *Peacock* after their months in the tropics.

The men visited the old Carmel Mission which was nearly in ruins after four or five years of the secularization program. They hunted small game in the vicinity of Monterey. And they discoursed with a strange type of American, the half-civilized mountain men who had drifted to this western limit of the continent.

It cannot be said with certainty that Commodore Kennedy appreciated the political implications of the California situation when he arrived at Monterey, or even when *Peacock* departed a week later. Some contemporary observers have stated flatly that he tried to persuade the rebellious Californians to seek admission as a State of the North American Union. A recent American historian presents evidence and his conjecture that the commodore was guilty of trying to provoke a quarrel with the provincial governor.

It is difficult to establish precisely what occurred during the incident commonly referred to as the Alvarado Revolt. Historian Hittell wrote, "No people in the world, perhaps, have been more addicted to grandiloquent appeals, proclamations, *pronunciamientos* and all that kind of inflammatory literature than the Mexicans; and the Californians were Mexicans." A scrutiny of the comments made by Americans and other *Anglos* regarding this same affair raises a question as to which group excelled in confusing the issue.

No independent nation or new American State came into being because of this successful revolt. Probably no more than 200 men were involved on both sides of the conflict. Few of these were experienced fighting men. No one really wished to shed any blood. As a matter of fact, the central and southern areas of Alta California could not have been aware of the physical act of revolt until perhaps a week after it had occurred.

Yet one likely result of this internal quarrel may have been overlooked by historians. The point could be made that when the few revolutionaries declared California to be a free and sovereign State, even though their loyalty remained with the Republic of

Mexico, they were never again fully Mexican in spirit. The general congenial attitude of the *Californios* six years and ten years later in the face of outright American military occupation tends to lend weight to such a thesis.

Because it has been so indifferently remembered, and because it bears so directly upon this story, the Revolution of 1836 is worthy of consideration here.

That portion of the log of Sloop *Peacock* for October 26, as quoted earlier, included a reference to the 21 gun salute at the sun's meridian. It was noted that the Fort returned the salute. This would have been normal. *El Castillo* was equipped with heavy guns and was maintained as an active military station. It is not especially important, but the precise accuracy of the ship's log may be questioned. Consider this excerpt from the narrative written by Fleet Surgeon Ruschenberger.

> The government of Upper California is, at present, administered by Lieutenant Colonel Don Nicolas Gutierrez. Don Nicolas resides at the presidio, or garrison, where he commands, without other assistance than that of a major of artillery, a captain and a lieutenant of infantry, and one or two corporals, fourteen men, and two field pieces. At the time of our visit they were nightly on guard, expecting an attack from some disaffected rancheros (farmers) and Indians. The day after our arrival we saluted the place, which was regularly acknowledged from the garrison. The whole military force of Upper California does not exceed one hundred and fifty men.

This was probably an accurate statement by a foreign visitor not involved in the strong passions of the time and place. Certainly nine days later, and probably sooner, the fort was not manned. This was in response to the order of Gutiérrez. And his intention was that all the powder was to be removed to the presidio garrison.

The origin and very heart of Spanish Monterey was the Presidio and first mission complex founded by Serra and Portolá in 1770 and christened San Carlos Borromeo de Monterey. By 1836 some parts of the garrison had disintegrated into virtual ruins; yet the presidio chapel tower still dominated the little village of adobe houses scattered across the rolling plain toward the fort on the hill a mile to the northwest.

The Presidio had been constructed at the bottom of the fishhook loop often used to discribe the shoreline of Monterey Peninsula. An estuary had been formed there where the converging streams draining the semi-circle of low hills on the south met the waves and tides of the Bay.

The fort had been constructed well down the broad nose of a descending ridge where its guns could command the roadstead and the village. In 1827, with the increase in maritime commerce following the Spanish repression of such foreign contacts, the Californians had built a Custom House, near the shore and perhaps a quarter mile southeast of *El Castillo*.

In the spring of 1836 the government at Mexico City sent the politically inept Colonel Chico to be Governor of California. The revolutionary reforms he promptly attempted to initiate were considered radical and unnecessary by the local people.

During the several months of his administration Governor Mariano Chico had brought down upon his head much trouble and scandal throughout the entire province. Probably the best thing he did for the Californians and himself was to board a vessel for Mexico at the end of July 1836. He never returned. The well-meaning, reasonably competent Nicolas Gutiérrez then found himself for the second time the acting Governor. He was a native of Spain and a soldier who took seriously what he assumed to be his duty. Both conditions were probably a deterrent to his happiness and success in a job he never seemed to have desired.

The primary irritation among the few leading Californians of this time was the dominance of the centralist party in Mexico. In brief, this meant that Alta California was to be treated as a department of government, supervised by an appointee of the central government, and being something less politically self-sufficient than a territory would have been. In respect to monetary assistance flowing from California to Mexico City or vice-versa it appears that the respective contributions were about equal since they were generally non-existent in either case.

Juan Bautista Alvarado and his uncle of eight years seniority, Mariano Guadalupe Vallejo, were born in Monterey. Alvarado, 27 years of age in 1836, was recognized as an able young man of considerable potential. José Castro of San Juan Bautista was undoubtedly the strong man of the northern region. Around Santa Barbara and in the Department of Los Angeles other strong leaders from among the old families quite often acted as though this province had no capital at Monterey where the elected *diputacion* or assembly duly met and prescribed governing *reglamentos*.

Mexican California was a vast area of lonely ranchos, thinly settled by a courageous people who seemed to have been perfectly happy with their simple pastoral culture. They would have fought for their beloved land against any reasonable odds even with their archaic weapons. But foreigners had infiltrated within and could bring overwhelming force by the sea. The *Californios* were few in number and their inter-communication could move no faster than a saddle horse or coastwise sailing vessel.

A personal quarrel between government clerk Alvarado and Gutiérrez, involving official accounting and the latter's duty-bound support of the centralist party directives, led to a condition of planned insurrection by the time the *Peacock* dropped anchor at Monterey. Young Alvarado suddenly found himself a general without ever having been a soldier. Vallejo prudently sat out this rebellion in Pueblo Sonoma until it had succeeded. José Castro was not only the prime military leader, he was made president of the new *diputacion*. Alvarado accepted or requested the assistance of possibly some 50 *Anglo* woodcutters and residents of dubious status of the Santa Cruz-Monterey area. These frontiersmen with their long rifles and easy consciences were unquestionably the core of his attack force. But in a few years time he had good reason to regret ever having become obligated to them in this manner.

On the night of November 3rd, the rebels quietly infiltrated the little town of some 500 citizens. They surrounded the presidio, found the fort deserted, and searched desperately to gather enough gunpowder to load one cannon with a ball. There are several different stories about the size of the cannon and when it was fired and from where. Fired it was, when a parley of war the next day between the rebels and the Governor elicited only his refusal to surrender. But he did recognize his situation and surrendered a few hours after the one lucky shot blew some tile off the roof of the Governor's presidio quarters.

A few days later the hapless Gutiérrez was shipped off to Mexico with some of his aides. It was not long before the natural leadership qualities of Alvarado caused him to be seated in the Governor's chair and recognized by Mexico, essentially because the central government was too preoccupied elsewhere to do otherwise.

The *diputacion* met on November 6 and the two following days. They declared that Alta California would remain a free, sovereign State, independent of Mexico, until the hated centralist government was removed. Several proclamations to this effect were issued and the news started moving among the ranchos.

Someone had fabricated a flag to symbolize the new sovereignty and freedom. The local United States faction is generally held responsible. The flag has been reported as having been raised; and also prevented from having been raised by a few cooler heads who saw this as a clear duplication of the Texas story.

On November 9, 1836, the respected Yankee merchant (not yet American Consul) Thomas Oliver Larkin penned a letter to his friend the respected Yankee merchant Abel Stearns at Pueblo Los Angeles. Most of the letter referred to the "Revolution" of five days earlier. It said in part:

> This will for a long time cause unsettled times in California. We must however get along as we can. The flag is to be six stripes & one Star, they say. It has broke up all work here for the present. I wish it was ended, for times to go Smooth again.
>
> Yours in much hast,

There was indeed a flag. It was made of crude white cloth bearing a single red star. This Alvarado flag currently may be seen at the Southwest Museum of Los Angeles.

In those pleasant fall days of 1836 the United States warship *Peacock* had been lying in the roadstead, perhaps a hundred yards off the Custom House. Much fresh water was brought aboard, and such supplies as a bullock, cheese, beans and potatoes, flour and pork, and clean sand. Repairs were made on spars, booms and sails. Breezes were light and weather clear. So reports the log of *Peacock*, watch by watch.

On Monday morning, October 31, the crew "hove up the anchor, made sail and stood out of the Bay of Monterey." On this day there was a very dense fog and light winds. The ship's cutter was put overboard, apparently to take soundings. At times a gun was fired for a signal and bearing. The following day was occupied in clearing Point Pinos. The merchant frigate *Rasselas*, Captain J. O. Carter, was visible at times also trying to clear the Bay.

Before the *Peacock* had departed, Commodore Kennedy received a letter dated Monte-Rey, Upper California, October 28th, 1836. It was signed by 13 "American Residents, Masters and Supercargoes of American vessels in Monte-Rey." Nathan Spear, Larkin and William Hinckley were among those signing. The letter expressed their "humble and grateful thanks for the lively interest you have been pleased to manifest for our commerce on this coast . . . The appearance of a U.S. ship of war on this coast, after so long an interval, and after so long an intercourse between our vessels and this territory, has been highly salutary. . . ."

Historian George Tays had some strong personal suspicion of the actual intentions of Commodore Kennedy during this week long ago in the little capital village of a foreign land. After having discovered certain confidential letters and documents in Mexican Archives, Tays authored an article in *California Historical Society Quarterly* of June 1933. He says that his writing revealed them publicly for the first time.

If Commodore Kennedy did not in fact hope to provoke the harassed Governor Gutiérrez into some physical or diplomatic reaction that would have offered an excuse for a counter response, he was at least guilty of an ill-mannered and undiplomatic approach to his official duties. There is no record among original source documents or the comments of historians to indicate that the visiting foreign naval officer of high rank had traveled the several hundred yards from his floating fortress to the Presidio to pay a courtesy call upon the military *comandante* and political chief of Alta California.

If Kennedy did meet Gutiérrez, he must have avoided any personal conversations dealing with the declared object of his visit. Instead, he prepared and transmitted three lengthy letters respectively on the 27th, 28th and 29th of October. The letters contained detailed charges of alleged abuses suffered by Americans in California.

Historian Tays, with the advantage of retrospect can pretty thoroughly demolish the substance of each charge. In fact, the studied, subdued replies of the beleagured Gutiérrez should have caused Kennedy to have investigated more deeply into his very serious accusations.

In respect to the ship *Rasselas*, as one example, Captain Carter obviously told the Commodore that he had been ordered to put to sea "after having satisfied or given a bond for the anchorage charges in port." Without investigating the accuracy of the complaint, Kennedy informed Gutiérrez, "I for my part have told Captain Carter to stay here as long as he deems convenient in order to finish his business."

The Governor coolly responded to this gunboat diplomacy by stating that Carter had refused to pay the anchorage and tonnage fee, had requested an eight day period to repair his ship, and that that time had now expired.

On the 29th, Gutiérrez transmitted the last letter in this exchange. He was extremely polite and formal as he listed in respect to each complaint just what official steps should have been taken to rectify the alleged injustices.

Kennedy had said in his letter of the 29th that there were notable differences in two of the cases, "which I cannot now investigate, as I find it necessary to visit Santa Barbara and other ports of this coast . . . "

The reason for this comment will undoubtedly remain a mystery. Tays asked why the call at Santa Barbara was necessary and then erroneously assumed it did occur. The log of *Peacock* is irrefutable. The ship's company could see land on the larboard side each day of the 13 day voyage to Mazatlán. There were no intermediate ports of call.

Tays reports that Gutiérrez indicated to his Secretary of War by letter of November 30, 1836, the idea that Kennedy might have taken California.

A letter dated a month later from the Governor's secretary, Navarrete, to a friend in Mazatlán declared, "He [Kennedy] acquainted himself fully about the revolution that was being plotted." Five years after the event the French intelligence agent Duflot de Mofras, who picked up all the gossip and (fortunately for historians) reported it in book form, stated that the Americans around Monterey were agitating to have California made a State of the American Union and that the *Peacock* officers were involved.

In 1836 John Clar, a junior American naval officer of Spanish heritage, commodore's interpreter and private clerk, was 23 years of age. It is difficult to imagine any more likely or competent ship's officer that could have been designated to communicate with the revolutionaries Alvarado and Castro.

Many years later Clar prepared a memorandum for the use of Historian Theodore Hittell. Much too briefly he described the visit of 1836 and two other California experiences of six years later. The former commodore's private clerk was explicit in declaring that he "always acted as interpreter between my commanders and the foreign functionaries." To emphasize his responsibility in 1836 he stated that "Mr. Thomas O. Larkin had just then arrived in this Country."

In the Memo he gave no indication that there had been any communication between Commodore Kennedy and the plotting Californians. Actually, Alvarado was very likely out in the country-side during those days, enlisting support for his cause. Nor did Historian Hittell apparently deem the rare presence of an American warship in Monterey Harbor to be of enough importance to report in his description of the Alvarado Revolt.

In respect to the complaints of Americans which caused the official confrontation between Gutiérrez and Kennedy, Clar mentioned the alleged impressment of American citizens into the local army. The Governor returned "very explicit answers." In this case, he stated that some Americans were engaged as civil guards but never as soldiers. Captain Carter's direct complaint to Kennedy was also mentioned.

Another, and probably more aggravated complaint described in this Memo involved the prohibition against whaling vessels being "allowed to dispose of part of their cargoes in order to pay for refreshments [provisions]. . . or make any traffic denied to other vessels. . . unless Custom House duties were paid."

All of this brought on "quite an animated correspondence" until the Governor, "being the feeblest had to yield to circumstances, and finally concluded that he would report the matter to the Government at Mexico. . ."[1]

Historian Tays asks if one can doubt that Commodore Kennedy would have liked to have been instrumental in acquiring California for the United States. It would seem that there yet remain some legitimate doubts, at least in respect to his behavior at Monterey in 1836.

The *Peacock* called at Mazatlán, then San Blas. At the end of November they were in Acapulco. Some typhoid fever touched the crew. In January they were at Lima, Peru. Chile and Peru were at war and American officials wished the *Peacock* to remain in this vicinity. Callao was the chief port of call for United States ships.

In March the *Peacock* sailed down to the Island of Juan Fernandez and then returned. Then on the 5th of July they set sail

---

[1]The six-page, undated Memorandum is filed as manuscript C-B 1064 at Bancroft Library. Hittell referred to it as "Clar's MS."

Faxon D. Atherton, later capitalist, was also at Monterey in 1836 and apparently enjoying the action as a carefree youngster of 21 years. He made no reference whatever to U.S. Navy involvement. He said the rebels waved a flag but, unfortunately, he gave no description of the flag he says was raised at the taking of the Presidio. **California Diary**, pub. Cal. Hist. Soc., 1964, Doyce B. Nunis ed.

for home. In another month they rounded Cape Horn. With brief stops at Río de Janeiro and Bahia they progressed northward with a great longing for home.

On October 27, 1837, the Sloop *Peacock* anchored opposite the City of Norfolk, Virginia. They had been away more than two and one-half years, and plowed more than 54,000 miles of the world's oceans.

The ship *Peacock* was later assigned to work with the famous Wilkes Exploring Expedition. In 1840 at the mouth of the Columbia River the noble little vessel was totally wrecked and lost.

---

Six months after the Sloop *Peacock* reached Norfolk, John Clar was assigned to the recently launched Frigate *Columbia*. This was a 44-gun vessel, 175 feet in length and served by a complement of 480 men. On May 6th, 1838, the frigate and her consort sloop *John Adams* slipped away from Hampton Roads. This East India Squadron was commanded by Commodore George C. Read.

A rather dreary two-volume narrative describing the ensuing trip around the world was written by the frigate's chaplain. In it School Master John Clar was mentioned only once. This was in reference to his entertaining the ship's officers with his guitar.[5] Their course followed that of the *Peacock* voyage, except that the first port of call was the Portuguese Island of Madeira. Then the vessels sailed southwesterly to Río. In mid-August they rounded the Cape of Good Hope and by October the officers were entertaining the Sultan of Muscat in Arabia as a gesture of appreciation for favors received three years earlier by Sloop *Peacock*. Courtesy calls followed at Bombay, Goa and Colombo.

As the vessels sailed toward the west coast of Sumatra, preparations were made for battle action if necessary. Cutlasses, battle axes and pikes were sharpened. Officers and men engaged in target practice with muskets and pistols. There was some serious business to conduct with the Rajah of Kuala Batu.

In 1832, Commodore John Downes in the United States Frigate *Potomac* had delivered severe punishment to the Malay pirates of this vicinity for murdering the crew of the American

---

[5]Fitch W. Taylor, **Voyage Around the World** (N.Y., 1842). This long travelogue and sermon by the chaplain of **Columbia** tells little of the ship's company. It does give a valuable description of a "tar's" uniform with the comment that negligent dress incurred a penalty of half a dozen lashes, "and most frequently it is inflicted. This tends to render the appearance of the whole crew strikingly neat on the Sabbath."

ship *Friendship*. Now in August of 1838 by an act of treachery the captain and a seaman of Barque *Eclipse* had been killed and $2,000 in cash stolen.

The warships *Columbia* and *John Adams* came to anchor some 200 miles down the west coast of Sumatra near Meuké and Kuala Batu. It was the 20th day of December. Several local rajahs were brought into conversation regarding reimbursement of the stolen money and punishment for the guilty. Little resulted except evasive talk. The chief rajah protested his innocence and cited the problems of capturing the murderers.

In a few days both ships answered a time deadline by bombarding the forts of Kuala Batu. The cannonade was answered feebly by the Maylays. Then on the first day of the New Year of 1839, landing parties went ashore at Meuké after a bombardment and set fire to the flimsy town. By mid-January the rajahs were very anxious to enter treaties of perpetual friendship and respect.

In early February the squadron called at Singapore. Then they set sail for Macao and Canton. When the Frigate *Columbia* was anchored in the roads of Macao it had the appearance of a floating hospital. One hundred and twenty or more men were on the sick list, most of them suffering from dysentery.

Hoping that the disease would abate in more northern waters, they set sail for the Sandwich Islands. And in a few days the ships, and especially the frigate, were faced by another great peril. A raging typhoon almost carried the vessel onto a lee shore. Fortunately, the storm abated enough for them to claw off and pursue their eastward course. But much of the fresh provisions brought aboard had been ruined. This food and more temperate weather were the only treatments known to improve sufferers from tropical dysentery. The disease did not abate.

The ships became separated and sailed on alone. Some men died as the days passed, some recovered and others were taken sick. Before the *Columbia* anchored off Honolulu, twenty-six bodies had been consigned to their graves in the deep Pacific. On the day of landing, the 10th of October, another man was buried ashore. Sloop *John Adams* arrived forty days later.

In the Sandwich Islands French as well as British naval officials were maneuvering for local advantages with the Hawaiian royal family. Possibly to observe French activities the American squadron moved down to Tahiti. In January of 1840 they raised Valparaiso; then they coasted north to Callao, the harbor of Lima,

Peru. Callao seems to have been selected thereafter as the principal Pacific Coast base for United States naval operations. Then after rounding the "Cape of Terrors" the two vessels anchored at Hampton Roads in June, two years and one month after their departure.

The Naval School Master, now aged 27, called the City of Norfolk, Virginia, his place of residence. This he did long after he had departed permanently from that great naval base. Probably he was sent to Philadelphia to conduct shore classes when the *Columbia* cruise had ended. Although no proper naval academy existed, Philadelphia is recognized as the place of its inception.

On October 15, 1841, Navy Department Headquarters wrote to John Clar in care of Commodore Read at Philadelphia saying,

> Sir: You are hereby appointed a Professor of Mathematics ... and will proceed to Norfolk, without delay and report ... for duty on board the U.S. Sloop of War Cyane. Your compensations will be at the rate of twelve hundred dollars per annum ...

There was also enclosed an oath of office to be "taken and subscribed."

Naval Archives contain a Circular of Appointment transmitted by Secretary Upshur to the new professor and also a response from the latter declaring his desire to please. Professors of less than 12 years service probably ranked with Lieutenant Commanders.

Sloop *Cyane* registered 792 tons, was 132 feet long, and carried 18 guns. This vessel had been built in Boston only four years earlier. The name *Cyane* has commonly been borne by some American warship through all the years since John Paul Jones captured the first British sloop of that name.

On November 1, 1841, Commodore Thomas ap Catesby Jones came aboard *Cyane* at Norfolk for the short trip to Hampton Roads.[6] Here he probably boarded his frigate flagship for the voyage around South America to his new post as leader of the United States Pacific Squadron. Then Sloop *Cyane* beat out into the heavy weather of an Atlantic winter "with double-reefed top-

---

[6] Thomas ap Catesby Jones (1760-1858) was of Welsh origin. The ap is Welsh for "from" or "of". Correct pronunciation of Catesby is "Kate's-bee". In the early 1960's a fun society was formed in Monterey, using his name and reputation. At the cocktail-business meeting this writer was graciously welcomed as the honored mystery guest. Beyond their fun, this society served the useful purpose of goading the conscience of too many Californians (**and** the Navy) who readily honor Sloat and the Bear Flaggers for doing exactly what Jones did at an earlier date. The name Cyane is pronounced "Sigh-an."

sails and wallowing like a gutter snipe." Commander C.K. Stribling was master. They pushed southward in some fair weather and much foul. And by mid-December the sloop entered Río de Janeiro harbor. In the Hittell Memo Clar wrote, "On this voyage I was the Professor of Mathematics and navigator, but always acted as interpreter with foreign functionaries."

Several popular accounts and volumes of official documents describe many events occurring during this cruise of the *Cyane* and its associated American ships of war. Commodore Jones was unquestionably following orders, secret or otherwise. And in doing so he found it necessary to deflect his nation's embarrassment onto his own person.

A political crisis was clearly developing in respect to the Sandwich Islands and Mexican California. Old Mexico seemed to be in a state of constant turbulence. The France of Louis Philipe was insinuating itself deeply into Mexican affairs.

While *Cyane* was laboring down the coast of South America the Russians began their physical withdrawal from the easy-going, undeveloped Province of Alta California. As might be expected, that action merely served to intensify the cat and mouse game between England and the United States. And at this time, above the Rio Grande the Texians were nearing a state of rebellion against the sovereign Mexican Government.

Fleet Surgeon William Maxwell Wood was in the U. S. Pacific Squadron in 1844. He wrote a book which contains many biased opinions but also many valuable comments about the places and times. Also available are the brief personal letters of Midshipman Alonzo C. Jackson, who was aboard the Frigate *United States* during the very similar action under Commodore Sloat just four years following this cruise of *Cyane*. The Jackson letters also contain pertinent comments, especially as seen through the eyes of a young fighting cock. The youngsters of his breed generally took out their frustrations by fighting duels among themselves. And it must be reported in passing that most of their superiors did little to curb such unnecessary bloodletting.

But most important for this story, there is available the fascinating "Journal of a Cruise to California and the Sandwich Islands on Board the U.S.S. *Cyane* . . . ," kept by Acting Gunner William H. Meyers. With eye-witness personal records so everlastingly vibrant with life there is little need to refer to formal government depositions made by Commodore Jones and other officials.

Gunner Meyers obviously possessed an intelligence and education far beyond that of the average enlisted seaman of his time. His thick personal journal and sketches record the rugged life and privations suffered in this twilight era of wooden ships of war. The unending search for strong drink, the bloody backs under the cat-o-nine tails for the most common infractions of discipline, the shipboard gossip and the precious bits of vital history are described there with salty humor.

From several entries in the journal it would appear that the 26 year-old Meyers and the 28 year-old professor became congenial shipmates on Sloop *Cyane*. The first record of their meeting was a journal entry of Sunday, November 21: "repaired to the forecastle and smoked a few segars with Mr. Clar and Dr. A.Y.P. Garnett. . . . " And off the coast of Brazil one pleasant moonlit night Meyers wrote, " . . . had a dissertation with Professor Clar and [Lieutenant] Middleton, left them firmly impressed with an idea that whatever is, is right, at eleven o'clock turned in . . . " Again on December 15, at Río de Janeiro: "Went ashore with Mr. Clare and Doct. Garnette."

In mid-January of 1842 *Cyane* rounded the "much dreaded Cape Horn," as Meyers put it. By the end of the month they had reached Valparaiso. For the following seven months this vessel and three or four other ships of the Pacific Squadron cruised the west coast of South America. Commodore Jones flew his broad pennant at the masthead of Frigate *United States*.

*Cyane* spent much of July 1842 in the port of Coquimbo, which is about 200 miles north of Valparaiso. Meyers described a social event which occurred in that harbor on the evening of July 10th on board Sloop *Cyane*. His flippant observation is of special value for this biographical sketch. Nowhere else among the existing records of John Clar does the austere professor become so human, even with proper allowance made for the sarcasm of a fun-loving sailor.

Meyers told of the "awful preparations" being made all morning to decorate the poop deck and screen it from the gaze of the vulgar. Then about noon the ship's boats began transporting ladies and gentlemen from the city. Came a band of musicians from the frigate. Commodore Jones and his officers with all their gilt and epaulettes began to parade the deck. Sleep was out of the question, wrote Meyers, so he came on deck.

"There I beheld our old purser and two old fat ladies attempting to find room to promenade the decks together . . . Smirking reefers [midshipmen], would-be wise doctors, and *even our democratic professor*, perambulating the short distance from the poop to the forecastle and endeavoring to do himself brown in their estimation. . . . Each looked as if he thought himself the particular object of admiration. . . . Nobody was tight, oh no, certainly not."

| Commodore Full Dress | Purser Undress | Surgeon Full Dress | Lieutenant Full Dress | 1st Ass't Engineer Full Dress |

UNITED STATES NAVY, 1841

# 3 We Raised
## the Glorious Stars and Stripes

*O*n early September *Cyane* was at Callao with the *United States*, Sloop *Dale* and Schooner *Shark*. The 16 gun Sloop *Yorktown* was cruising farther south. Rumors and facts regarding actions and intended actions on the part of foreign powers were common gossip now, and undoubtedly also the prime subject of official dispatches.

Fleet Surgeon Wood wrote, "For many years before California was annexed, the impression seemed to exist in the United States Pacific squadron that its most important purpose was to occupy California . . . The British squadron seemed to have an equally strong idea that its business was to prevent any such act on the part of ours, and consequently these squadrons went about watching each other."[7]

In late August of 1842 a British Rear Admiral arrived at Callao. Senior naval officers of both nations dined on his flagship. But news from several sources, including an American consul, was leading Jones to believe that Mexico and the United States had at last come to a state of war. There was also a rumor that Mexico had indeed ceded Alta California to Great Britain. Then on September 5 the British flagship quietly departed under its own secret orders.

At a conference of ship's captains with the Commodore it was agreed that the American squadron must take and hold California immediately.

So the *United States* and *Cyane* hastily took on supplies, including picks and shovels for the purpose of providing earthworks in the event they were called upon to resist a British landing party behind them. The ships crowded on sail on September 7th and drove northward. Sloop *Dale* was diverted to Panama for the transmittal of official dispatches to Washington. Navigator Clar recalled, "Of course, no one except the Commanders knew where we were going."

---

[7]William Maxwell Wood, **Wandering Sketches of People and Things** (Phila., 1849).
See also, "The Conquest of California," from the letters of Alonzo C. Jackson in the Coe Collection, Yale.

Along the way water casks were dropped overboard and used for targets by the big guns. The marines engaged in musket practice by firing at bottles tied to the yards. Cutlasses were sharpened and sand made ready to spread on the decks when time for bloody battle action arrived.

The American ships anchored off Monterey on the evening of October 18. The next day they beat their way into the harbor against a wind. The ships came in flying the white English naval ensign (as did Sloat at the conquest of 1846). Anchors were dropped in such a manner that the ships could be swung for action against the town and the fort on the hill, or against British warships which were believed to be close behind.

"On the 19th October, 1842, Governor Alvarado was summoned to surrender the place to the American forces," wrote Professor Clar in his Memo. "This summons was peremptory; there was no time for hesitation."

A Mexican barque in the harbor was captured as a prize of war (much to the delight of Meyers since crewmen enjoyed a portion of prize sales in those days). It is to be noted for the moment that one passenger (and therefore a prisoner of war) on this ship was the young Señorita María Jesús Estudillo. Her people were large grant holders in the San Leandro area. Her probable importance in the story ahead will be observed later.

On October 19, Gunner Meyers made this journal entry:

> Got up battle lanthorns [lanterns] axes, spunges, and rammers, in fighting trim, cleared away the guns, grape, round and cannister on deck. Sanded the decks. Hoisted out the cutter, match ready, etc. Strong lights at the fort. . . . At 8 turned in for a nap before I am popped out of this world.

For both a description of Alta California's capital city in this era and a justification of Jones' 1842 action, the later words of Fleet Surgeon Wood are pertinent. He wrote:

> In the fall of 1844, we lay in the harbor of Monterey, ready to take California upon the first intelligence justifying it; in 1845 we did the same thing, and in 1846 it was taken. . . . On a hill to the left of the town stood a farcical structure, called a fort, with a Mexican flag flying. It has much the appearance of a cow-shed, standing on the hillside, with a low mud wall in front of that part facing the harbor.
>
> At this season, the country around Monterey presented to the eye naked, brown-clad hills, or open pine barrens, with here and there a clump of live oak trees. All was uninclosed and unculti-

vated; the only houses seen being the scattered whitewashed buildings of Monterey . . . and the population about a thousand.

Bullock pens stood on the sandy unpaved streets, and myriads of beef bones lay scattered in every direction, characteristic of the staple commodity of a place in which raw hide is current money at the rate of two dollars.

Neither Meyers nor Jackson, in 1842, held quite such a low opinion of the fort, *El Castillo*. Both went to the fort and reported the presence of 14 heavy guns, about a ton of powder and a good supply of brass and iron balls. The "cowshed" was a barracks and not the fort proper. The mud wall (as rediscovered in 1967) consisted of a thick adobe and stone redoubt.

And William Heath Davis (who could have been prejudiced for several reasons including the fact that in 1847 he married prisoner of war Señorita Estudillo) declared in his famous biographical history:

"Had Alvarado known of the coming of Jones beforehand, he would have made preparations to defend Monterey . . . by firing from the castle, as was done . . . in 1818 when two insurgent vessels manned by Spaniards from South America came into the harbor of Monterey. . ."

Historian T. H. Hittell also stated that the ailing Governor Alvarado first thought of offering resistance, but then realized the overwhelming strength represented by some 800 American fighting men.[8]

At any rate, the *Californios* were thunderstruck at the demand to surrender. Alvarado visited Jones aboard the frigate and then went to his Salinas rancho rather than personally suffer the indignity of yielding. From there he sent a message to Los Angeles where his appointed successor, Manual Micheltorena, had hesitated on his way from Mexico. The new Governor chose to remain in the southern pueblo and shout defiance at the brigand Americans. It

[8]William Heath Davis, **Sixty Years in California** (1889). Davis first saw California in 1831, died in Oakland in 1909. This reminiscence of a long life is a very valuable historical record. It is unquestionably subject to some personal bias and error of fact. Davis gives an account of his conversation with Jones a few days after the capture. He states that the affable commodore was quite frank in declaring his prime mission was the prevention of England's acquisition of California. The "insurgent vessels" were those of Bouchard, mentioned earlier.

T.H. Hittell (**Hist.** vol 2, 320) notes that he depended chiefly upon Clar's eyewitness account of the Jones' Incident. The historian visited the San Francisco Clar home to discuss such events, according to the personal recollection of this writer's father. In the Memo he wrote for Hittell, John Clar referred to the incident as "this harmless conquest." He also noted that Jones appointed "civil magistrates" but failed to mention his own designation as Secretary of State.

is questionable whether Alvarado himself would not have preferred American occupation rather than a new political appointee of unknown character from Mexico.

Meyers noted that the morning of Thursday, October 20, 1842, was foggy.

> Opened arms chests, distributed pistols, muskets and ball cartridges, filled marine cartouch boxes. At ½ past 9 five boats from frigate and 4 from us, commanded by Captain Stribling containing about 70 marines and 200 seamen and officers pulled for the landing. Beat to quarters and hauled down the flag of truce. In about 20 minutes after landing the Mexican flag was hauled down and United States flag hoisted with three cheers. . . .
> Sentinels on shore and at the fort and town. Lieut Delaney Commandante of the fort     Capt Stribling [is] Military governor    Lockwood, professor of Mathematics of the frigate [is] Adjt general[.] Mr. Clar Secty of West California. . . . The fort dubbed Fort Catesby—bah.

The professor, and first Secretary of State of American California, himself wrote in the mentioned Kenady letter, 41 years later:

> . . . in 1842 under Com. Jones we hoisted the glorious Stars and Stripes in Monterey four years before the [Mexican] war. In the intercourse with foreign peoples I was generally the spokesman. At our taking of the fort the functionary in charge tendered me the keys—but with native modesty I pointed out my Commander Stribling as the proper magnate.

Unfortunately, a little less native modesty and more of Meyers' tart effusiveness could have been of far more value to posterity in view of the wonderful story this man could have told. Hittell says, "He [Clar] acted as interpreter between the United States and Californian authorities in the Monterey business." That statement implies more than it should. Thomas Oliver Larkin and also the scholarly Mexican citizen William Hartnell represented both governments as interpreters. Jones' secretary, Henry La Reintree, must definitely have been at the Commodore's side here and later at Sonoma and Pueblo Los Angeles.

No doubt the "functionary in charge," was one Captain Mariano Silva. He could indeed have been first addressed by Professor Clar at the fort. And on the designated staff constituting the American military government it was imperative that someone fluent in Spanish should have been constantly available.

Taking of Monterey, 1842, from Meyers' Journal

The following day, October 21st, principally through the good work of Larkin, it was agreed by all that a state of war did not exist. The Mexican flag was raised and formally saluted. Gunner Meyers expressed the situation as viewed by the men below decks with the following journal entry on October 21:

> So perish all my greatness, adieu my visions of prise money, I am dumb henceforth. Loaded the guns in silence. Reembarked the Ex Govnr, Secty, Marines and Seamen. Mr. Jones, Midn & Corporal Angel drunk. At 8 reported battery. So ends the Capture.

Alvarado sent word to Micheltorena. Commodore Jones awaited the arrival of the Governor and his rag-tag army which was to cause a great deal more resentment among the local residents than had been generated by the overwhelming yet rigidly disciplined Americans. But Micheltorena did not come to Monterey.

About a year after this incident Larkin was appointed American Consul at Monterey. In what was probably his first official letter to Washington he told of the good will of all parties at the provincial capital. The Capture, which had occurred 18 months earlier, was still an issue of diplomatic concern. In this respect Larkin wrote: "It was the opinion of many, both Natives and Foreigners in 1842 that the taking of Monterey by Com. Jones would be a serious injury to his country. . . . I am happy to give as my opinion that the result has not been as anticipated, in fact, I think it proved to be the reverse."

On Friday, November 18, Meyers noted: "General invitation to the officers ball at Larkin's, I suppose a grand case of seduction."

A week later Mr. Larkin's half-brother, John B. R. Cooper, entertained the ship's company at his home in Monterey. Presumably Gunner Meyers was one of the guests. Cooper was a naturalized Mexican citizen and the brother-in-law of Colonel Vallejo of Sonoma.

Between those two social events Meyers noted that seven of the crew received "9 lashes of the cats" for drunkeness, and another man 12 for smuggling liquor aboard. There was nothing unusual in this except that one of the drunks was Anderson Norris, Negro cook of the *Cyane*. It is quite possible that this degradation led to desertion, death, and a small share of immortality for Norris before two month's time had elapsed.

Micheltorena showed no inclination to occupy his capital city so long as a powerful and probably rather popular foreign military force was in the community. So Jones coasted up to San Francisco Bay where the *Cyane* dropped anchor "4 miles dist. from the town of Yerba Buena" on December 12, 1842. If the silent rolling hills of grass and sage that day gave forth any divination of the future for young Professor Clar, he would have sensed that a full half of his entire life span was to be spent here. It is more likely that in the eyes of the far wandering citizen of Virginia this was but another foreign seaport and rather unpromising one, in all truth, except for its excellent harbor.

Said Gunner Meyers, "Plenty of deer about looking at the ship with wonder. This is a magnificent bay indeed, but they have queer names for things."

A decade earlier the able Governor Figueroa had recognized the anchorage hazard at the Presidio and called for plans for a townsite and wharf at Yerba Buena Cove some three leagues around the peninsula point. Captain William Richardson from up near Mission San Rafael had heeded the governor's request and proceeded with the construction of a store and a few frame structures in the years following 1835.

Most of the rare visitors coming into San Francisco Bay preferred the firm anchorage west of Angel Island where they were assured of easy access to fuel wood, excellent water, fresh meat and other supplies, and hunting and pleasant companionship ashore. On December 13 the *Cyane* moved and "came to anchor in South Soleta [Sausalito] in 3½ fathom water."

It would seem that Jones had come to San Francisco Bay for two reasons. This was an ideal place to refit and repair sea-weary vessels, and careen them if necessary on the shallow mud flats. Also it would not be unlikely that Commodore Jones could have been attempting to improve international relations during this particularly embarrassing interim before his meeting with Governor Micheltorena.

To accomplish the latter, the Commodore and a select party traveled north and east about 35 miles to Pueblo Sonoma for a visit with Mariano G. Vallejo, Military Comandante of the Province of Alta California. On December 23rd, Meyers entered in his journal, " . . . Jones and suite returned from this visit to Colonel Vallejos at St. Omer, [Sonoma] absent 6 days."

It is not known if John Clar traveled with the party as interpreter. Vallejo, in his own records, makes no mention of this point. It would certainly seem that the Commodore would hardly have

dared venture into such a delicate situation without a trustworthy interpreter. On the other hand, the very fact that Clar would undoubtedly have revealed himself as a native of Spain could have made him for this reason more suspect than the Yankees and English whom Vallejo deliberately cultivated because of their ingenuity and energy. For a time after the period of the 1822 revolution, Mexican citizens of Spanish birth were not implicitly trusted by their native born California neighbors.

Vallejo returned the visit on December 27, and received a 13-gun salute from the *Cyane* as he boarded her at Sausalito. On the 29th, Captain Richardson and a large local party came aboard and the ship weighed anchor for Monterey where a grand New Year's party was held at the Governor's residence.

Then the *Cyane* sailed down the coast to carry Jones to an arranged meeting with Micheltorena at Pueblo Los Angeles. On January 18 the ship anchored at San Pedro roadstead and the Commodore took with him a party of eight, apparently not including John Clar, on the inland journey for a three-day conference.

Then the *Cyane* coasted down to Mazatlán where she stayed until the 15th of March. On April 12 the ship anchored in the port of Monterey again.

On April 15, 1843, Meyers made an entry in his journal which, standing alone, is rather confusing in respect to time and place. It is quoted as follows, "Heard that Anderson Norris was killed whilst heading a band of Indians. Francis not taken. Rogers a prisoner." Francis was a seaman, and James Rogers was listed on the ship's roster as "Boy, 1st Class." Later Rogers was returned to the *Cyane* and flogged with 12 lashes of the cat-o-nine-tails for desertion, a very mild punishment presumably out of regard for his tender age.

This particular desertion had occurred while the ship was recently anchored at Sausalito. Such a common occurrence had not been impressive enough at the moment to be worthy of journal entry by Gunner Meyers. The fact of Norris's death and Rogers'

THE FUTURE CITY OF SAN FRANCISCO AS FIRST SEEN BY JOHN CLAR
Yerba Buena as sketched from the deck of the U.S.S. **Cyane** by Gunner William H. Meyers. The structures at the water edge are located along present Montgomery Street. The far right building could have been at about Sansome and Jackson. At low tide this shoreline was a mud flat.

Two harmless assumptions can be made about this picture. Professor Clar might well have been at the side of his friend and shipmate during its making. Secondly, the morning of Sunday, April 30, 1843, was a logical time for its creation. The hills of San Francisco are painted in the vivid green of spring in the original sketch, and not the drab brown they would have been the prior December when **Cyane** was anchored near "South Soleta." **Cyane** had been away from San Francisco Bay during 1843 until Thursday, April 26. That day she came to anchor "in 11 fathom water opposite the town of Yerba Buena." The weather was generally cold or windy until

Sunday the 30th. That day Meyers wrote: **Fine weather. Divine services as usual. 12 dinner. Went on shore . . . Visited the Billiard room. Saw a dog and cat fight. Heard lots of bear yarns Etc. At sundown came on board.**

Incidentally, Robert Ridley's Liquor and Billiard Saloon stood near the corner of later Clay and Kearney streets. On Monday the ship was moved to Sausalito.

reported capture was real news. Of much more interest at the present day is the importance indirectly attached to the death of Anderson Norris by Historian T. H. Hittell. To him it appeared to enter strongly upon the Bear Flag Revolution of three and one-half years later.

Meyers reported the later sequence of events as follows. On April 26, 1843, he noted the *Cyane* "came to an anchor in 11 fathom water opposite town of Yerba Buena." On a cold May 3rd: "Lieut. Shattuck and Mr. Clar went to St. Omar." On the next day he noted, "Heard for a fact that Norris was murdered by Salvador Vallejo." On Friday, May 12, "Cold and windy. Dispatches to St. Omar respecting the murder of Norris."

On May 13, Meyers went grizzly bear hunting on Angel Island. On the 27th the *Cyane* set sail for Monterey, after a full month in San Francisco Bay.

Hittell drew a relationship between the Norris incident and the Bear Flaggers through the hatred of Ezekial Merritt for Salvador Vallejo. There is obvious logic in the proposition although it is difficult to believe that the rough and rowdy American frontiersman Merritt needed any special inducement to assume the brash leadership of the insurgents of 1846.

Hittell gave his interpretation of this bit of history from a source of reference he noted as "Clar's MS." Mentioned twice by Clar but omitted by Hittell was reference to the great strength of Anderson Norris. This was alleged to be a major contributing factor leading to the use of arms against the *Cyane* cook. At any rate, in his Volume 2, page 426, the historian began telling of the incident by reference to Merritt. He wrote:

> In 1843, while he was pursuing his regular avocation of hunting and trapping in what is now Marin county, the United States sloop-of-war Cyane, Captain Stribling, ran into and for a short time lay at Saucelito for the purpose of refitting. While there a few of the sailors and among them a mulatto cook were allowed their liberty and a run on shore; but they become intoxicated and did not return by the time the vessel was ready to sail. The commodore thereupon requested Comandante Vallejo to apprehend the runaways and deliver them to the next American ship-of-war that might touch at San Francisco. Vallejo sent his brother Salvador to make the arrests. The latter found the cook at Merritt's camp and, according to Merritt's statement, shot him down in cold blood and the soldiers he had with him ran their swords through his body. Merritt, being a witness of the transaction, called Salva-

dor a murderer and declared that he would have him punished for his crime. Salvador angrily turned round, ordered him to shut up and struck him with a ramrod. In the presence of a squad of soldiers, Merritt could do nothing; but he vowed vengeance, and swore that, if he ever found an opportunity, he would slay Salvador on sight.

Quoting directly from Clar's Memo the story continues:

> I was sent with despatches to Commandante Vallejo at Sonoma in reference to the matter, and read to him the communication in Spanish. The Captain of our Ship (Stribling) demanded that Salvador Vallejo should be tried for murder, by law and duly punished unless he could prove that it was a justifiable homicide.
>
> Commandante Vallejo answered that his brother was no murderer, that our Cook was an extraordinarily strong man, seized some of their stacked arms, and was about to use them against the soldiers. At this, Salvador shot him and seeing the wound was mortal, to spare him further sufferings ordered his men to finish him.
>
> Captain Stribling reminded Vallejo that if justice was not done (and communication with Mexico required many months) the Americans here would take justice into their own hands.

Following this report of an incident in which he was a direct participant, Professor Clar offered to historian Hittell some hearsay information which the former must have believed was based upon fact.

Clar referred to the Bear Flag Insurrection, which had occurred, he declared somewhat enigmatically, "in the absence of ships of war." At any rate, during that action Merritt had been "Captain of a Company" and having Salvador "in his grip" would have killed him "but for the representations of Mr. Knight and others, that to kill Vallejo while his prisoner would damage the reputation of a noble hunter, etc. . . . Shortly after this Merritt died and this story is now almost forgotten."

After this particular visit to San Francisco Bay the *Cyane* called at Monterey for a few days and then coasted down to Santa Barbara. On June 24, 1843, she dropped anchor in San Diego harbor. Meyers noted the beautiful bay and fine weather. Otherwise — "For a description of the town, it is a miserable hole and the ugliest women I ever saw."

In early July *Cyane* touched at Mazatlán before sailing on to the Sandwich Islands. There seems to be little doubt that Jones was deliberately wandering about over his broad Pacific Station during these months so that his designated successor, Commodore

Dallas, could not find and relieve him of his command. Jones had received this public rebuke for the premature capture of California. Privately his action was probably commended.

On August 4 *Cyane* reached Honolulu and found frigates *Constellation* and *United States* there. The former, with Commodore Kearney, had entered the game of international politics by taking aboard the royal family to keep them and their land from domination by a too ambitious captain of a British sloop of war. Five months of technical domination by Great Britain here ended shortly thereafter when a higher ranking English naval officer arrived and restored the independent authority of the Hawaiian monarchy.

For Gunner Meyers, this Hawaiian adventure was a glorious, if illicit, romantic idyll when he became "the victim of the seducing wiles of the beautiful Maria Hilia," aged 14. Whether Professor Clar was an accessory before the fact, who would now dare to say? The evidence of record shows that Meyers failed in an attempt to borrow a little money from other approachable officers until Tuesday, October 3, 1843. In this last mention of his democratic friend he notes, "Fine weather. Employed at the guns. Borrowed thirty dollars from Mr. Clar."

After the Sandwich Island episode *Constellation* paid a visit to Monterey before rounding the Horn. On December 1, 1843, *Cyane* once more dropped anchor off Sausalito and stayed nine days. Then she coasted down to Callao on her homeward voyage.

But Professor Clar did not sail for home. In June he was transferred to the powerful Frigate *Savannah*, 44 guns and 480 men, flying the broad pennant of Commodore John D. Sloat, commander of naval forces of the United States in Pacific waters. The *Savannah* sailed back to the Sandwich Islands during the summer of 1844 and returned to Monterey before November, watching and waiting to see what pawns would next be moved in the tense international game.

With the mission system destroyed and no genuine direction or help coming from Old Mexico, the weak California government continued to deteriorate under the impact of aggressive foreign immigrants. Conquest was inevitable.

# 4  My Prospects are Indeed Gloomy

On March 22, 1845, on board Frigate *Savannah* in the harbor of Callao, Peru, Professor Clar wrote a letter making an official record of the state of his health, a condition already known to the recipient, Fleet Surgeon William Maxwell Wood. The petitioner asked that a survey of his condition be made so that if found proper he could return to the United States with as little delay as circumstances would allow.

Commodore John D. Sloat, over his elaborate signature, promptly ordered three fleet surgeons to make a strict and careful examination of the patient and report in duplicate copy. The result took the shape of a letter to the Commander of the Naval Forces of the Pacific Ocean signed by surgeons Wood, Grier and Wilson on March 25. (It is interesting that this action was recorded in the medical report as being performed in compliance with general instructions of the Secretary of the Navy issued as late as Oct. 25, 1843).

The doctors reported "that he is affected with frequent and severe spasms, was taken while on board this ship. His disease has been gradually increasing for the last three months, and will continue so long as he remains on ship board, so far as we can judge from appearances. We therefore recommend his immediate return to the United States."

On that same day the Commodore forwarded, through Captain James Armstrong, a letter telling Clar he was detached from Ship *Savannah*, given permission to return to the "U. States," and ordered to report immediately upon arrival to the Honorable Secretary.

This writer at different times has asked several physician friends to make a belated diagnosis from Naval Archives correspondence in this case. The patient was 32 years of age when affected, and he subsequently suffered these chest "spasms" for two years. In his advanced years he suffered from arthritis, but the earlier symptoms apparently did not reappear. The modern medical practitioners proposed asthma, rheumatic fever, and even neurosis as possible causes of the illness.

The patient was forced to spend six weeks at Valparaiso before he obtained passage on the American ship *Robin Hood*. Eighty-two days later he arrived in Boston. From there on July 30, 1845, he informed the Honorable Secretary, George Bancroft, of his presence, declared he had not recovered, and asked for a leave of absence.

Six weeks later the ailing professor was obviously becoming desperate. Again from Boston, on September 10th, he penned a two page letter, beautiful in penmanship and the literary form of that day. Fortunately, it contains a brief biographical record of the author's career as well as an historically valuable documentation of the direct and unsophisticated processes in this branch of government during its formative period.

Secretary Bancroft, the recipient, was recognized as a distinguished scholar, historian and diplomat. Unlike his successor of a year later Bancroft appears to have responded with sympathy to the unfortunate officer detached from duty and pay.

An enclosed opinion of a physician who judged "the condition of my system" indicated that the professor's disease was likely of long duration. Therefore, his services on ship board would be of hardly any advantage. And he would respectfully call the attention of the Chief Authority of the Navy "to the isolated situation in which my sickness has reduced me. From my rank of Professor I lose my pay while on shore, in addition to having lost my health when at sea. You will easily perceive by this, Sir, that if not relieved by some means or other, all my prospects are indeed gloomy."

The professor then suggested to the Honorable Secretary that perhaps some relief could be found in the rules and regulations for the better government of the Navy. Therein it was provided that disabled officers, seamen and marines might receive half pay. Or if the Secretary "knew of any situation of the Department Bureaux at Washington, or of anything elsewhere of your gift which does not require much mental exertion, nor affect the muscles of respiration, to which I am continually exposed when lecturing in my official capacity, I would willingly accept it, even though its salary should not be as lucrative as that of professors."

The letter was terminated with all the flourishes of that period:

I have the honor to be Sir
With great respect
Your Most Obt Servant
John Clar
Professor of Math.

On November 29, 1845, Secretary Bancroft wrote above his galloping signature the instruction to John Clar, Esq. that the two senior medical officers of Boston Navy Yard would make an examination of the patient upon the exhibition of his letter. They were to give an opinion of the degree of permanent disability in his case. He would then deliver the letter and the written report to the Officer of Commissioner of Pensions.

At this point there seems to have been a little bureaucratic confusion, or more likely a lack of official interest. Archives indicate that on March 18, 1846, the Honorable Secretary must again have personally responded to Clar's appeal. Three days later Commissioner of Pensions Edwards acknowledged the case and then apparently passed the decision on for Bancroft to make.

By the end of July a "lost or destroyed" order of pension, which had been issued on March 25, was acknowledged. Thereafter the ailing professor apparently received on the first day of each January and July the sum of 120 dollars. This was certainly one of the very earliest military sickness pensions paid by the United States. And it apparently was discontinued after a few months without any reinstatement of the pensioner to active duty.

In passing, it is of interest to note that the payroll sheet of Frigate *Constellation*, described earlier, also contained an indication of official policy in respect to government responsibility for the health of military personnel. One column of the sheet was headed "Amount of Hospital fund." After the name of John J. Clar on the roster was entered the sum of $4.89. This sum was deducted from his salary during 1832-34 as reimbursement for medical services rendered him on shipboard.

On October first, 1846, Clar wrote from Portsmouth, Virginia, to the new Navy Secretary, John Y. Mason, a citizen of Virginia and an eminently successful politician. He appears to have exhibited no official sympathy for the supplicant in this case.

The letter opened thus: "Sir, Being one of the unfortunate Professors of the Navy, who in addition to their forsaken condition, have for these fifteen months past suffered severely from a disease of the heart, contracted while on duty at sea. . . . "

Clar had been on shore more than a year and now the monthly pension was about to cease. He said that he was recovering from the severe reactions to the disease and therefore solicited some employment not requiring much mental exertion. He proposed a certain type of employment. Before consideration of that, however, the letter noted that Secretary Bancroft had offered Clar a professorship at the new Naval School at Annapolis upon his arrival a year earlier. Probably related to this offer is another archival document which undoubtedly represents the original scrawl of Cornelius K. Stribling. The half-page testimonial is undated. Commander Stribling deposed as follows:

> Mr. Clar served under my command between five and six years, I consider him a very competent teacher of Mathematics, French and Spanish; and if his health is sufficiently restored, would I have no doubt be a valuable acquisition to the Naval School. Mr. Clar is a gentleman of irreproachable character; and would I feel confident render good service in any situation in which he might be placed.

The Academy had opened, largely at the instigation of Bancroft, on October 10, 1845, at old Fort Severn. It is interesting to observe that a full course for naval officers at that period required a first and fifth year at the Academy, with the intervening three years at sea.

Now in the letter of October first to Secretary Mason, Clar referred to his understanding that some capable person was "wanted to attend to nautical instruments — the rating of chronometers, etc." He respectfully asked that he be placed under orders where he might obtain some pay.

On April 6, 1847, from Portsmouth, the professor formally advised Secretary Mason that he had recovered from his illness and had the honor to request orders for useful service.

Three weeks later Clar wrote a two-page letter, with the request that it be read at the Secretary's leisure. This was presented as a personal letter. Assuming that earlier suggestions had failed to reach the gentleman, the professor told of the cost of transporting delicate ships instruments to Washington for adjustment and repair and then back to the several naval yards. He also pointed out the maladjustment possible because of the unnecessary shaking during transportation and the subsequent hazard to vessels using them. The case of Sloop *Decatur* having erred more than 30 miles in navigation calculation during several days sailing because of a poorly adjusted chronometer was used as an example. It was also recommended that an exchange supply of chronometers should be kept at this place [Norfolk?] instead of requiring each ship to remove instruments for testing in Washington.

Clar complained that six months ago he had been promised an opportunity for employment when something was available. Now he had made a sound and valuable proposition. This proposal was also endorsed by the Commodore here, and furthermore, "other officers are paid whether employed or not, but my case is different . . . I have during these nearly two years of sickness spent the earnings of my past labours."

On May 10th, 1847, again from Portsmouth, Clar wrote to Secretary Mason regarding a communication he had received a week earlier. On April 23rd, Clar had appealed to the Bureau of Ordinance and Hydrology for a position at Gosport Navy Yard in which he might take charge of chronometers. The Secretary and Bureau Chief, however, agreed that the Master of the Yard or the officers of the vessels could attend to their chronometers adequately. Professor Clar now begged to state "with all due deference to the gentlemen of the Bureau" that they spoke from want of a correct knowledge, that the two recent Yard Masters were unlettered men totally unfit for such duties, that of two present ones it

*Mr Clar served under my command between five and six years. I consider him a very competent teacher of Mathematics, French and Spanish; and if his health is sufficiently restored would I have no doubt be a valuable acquisition to the Naval School.*

*Mr Clar is a gentleman of unreproachable character; and would I feel confident render good service in any situation in which he might be placed.*

C. K. Stribling
Commander, U.S.t

could be positively asserted that they lacked such ability and as proof thereof "all observations here are intrusted to the care of a Master's Mate — an irresponsible man, whose manifold duties alone while in charge of the Steamer *Engineer* prevents him from paying the requisite attention to such duties."

He named all of the names in the above citation, then he claimed that of new young masters of vessels, "few have ever seen the phasis of a chronometer, nor have they had any experience in the use of artificial horizons" and must depend on the instruments as received, and he had already cited the disastrous consequences which might follow.

It was plain that the professor was feeling very much imposed upon, suffering that special frustration of a self-confident technician in government service who is virtually ignored by political superiors. Furthermore, he was in fact an officer of the United States Navy ready for duty. Or perhaps he was less than an officer in the rigid scheme of rank. For, said he in concluding this letter to the Secretary, "If when on leave we professors are to get no pay, and when on application for duty we are to be denied orders, our existence in the service is entirely nugatory."

On September 2nd, 1847, after a lapse of five months since his last letter, the Professor told the Secretary in some 400 well-chosen words what he thought of treatment received and of Secretary John Y. Mason in particular. Thirty-six years later he wrote, "I was a veteran — applied for active service during the [Mexican] war — received magnificent promises but was forced to remain idle after a protracted illness. These promises were never accomplished, and in a moment of indignation damned the Secretary — asked him to strike my name from the rolls. . . ."

The letter of 1847 wasted neither ink nor time in declaring its intent. It began: "Sir, Your course toward me is one which for injustice, neglect, and underhand acrimony stands unprecedented in the annals of the Navy . . . you have on various occasions been pleased to tyrannize and worry me without a shadow of reason or even the least specious pretext." The Secretary was accused of giving his word to issue orders of employment on three specific occasions during the recent year, and of breaking his given word three times, even after various intellectual and accomplished officers had endorsed the proposed appointments.

"Lately, the Commander who goes to take charge of the Pacific Station has applied to you to have me ordered to go with him. His motives for doing so were on account of my experience in those seas, and my knowledge of the languages of the people of those regions, but you with habitual blindness to justice and utility, have once more denied me occupation, and disregarded his request."

Reference was made to the cessation of pay for off duty officers. "Here is an anomaly, a Navy officer without duty and without pay!" He accused the Secretary of not possessing the manly virtue of charging him openly to remove him from service, and "thus free me at once from the vile durance you have placed me under." Clar declared he had no political influence (which the Secretary knew) nor would he use it if he had, "but I shall not obsequiously cringe and ask you any favors. . . . Henceforth, I request you may consider as out of the reach of your orders Your very respectfully Ob't. Servant, John Clar."

It is possible that the professor's treatment was indeed unprecedented in that salty young Navy. Probably it has not often been surpassed in the long years since the Mexican War. At the same time, it would seem to be a reasonable conjecture that Navy Archives will reveal precious few letters from a junior officer to the Honorable Secretary of the Navy with as much beautifully flavored personal invective as graced this communication of September 2, 1847.

Attached to this last document in the file are a couple of notes barely legible. It would appear that an answer based on the notes was given which stated: "to remove all doubt the Department [that last word was struck out and "President" inserted instead] has directed his name be stricken from the rolls as a Prof of Math." Thus ended a proud and no doubt entirely honorable Navy career of 15 years. A new phase of John Clar's life was ready to begin in his thirty-fourth year.

# 5 The Argo Ship Humboldt

After he left the United States Navy, the greater part of John Clar's life was to be involved with land records rather than the sea. Yet one noteworthy sea voyage remains to be recounted.

As the young man's health improved he unquestionably found occupation as a railroad surveyor. In fact, greatly overblown family anecdote has him "building the Hoosac Tunnel." Very probably he did some preliminary route or earth moving computations there. The fact is that the great engineering marvel of the time, a railroad tunnel under Hoosac Mountain in Western Massachusetts, was begun about seven years after our hero had departed.

There is, in the archives of the Society of California Pioneers, an interesting handwritten document verifying the kind and the area of his employment. Although the signature is practically illegible the note clearly proclaims:

> This is to certify that the bearer Mr. John Clar is an Engineer of the Vermont and Massachusetts Railroad and that he is consequently entitled to pass free over the Fitchburg Railroad.
> Boston, June 28th, 1848

In the Kenady letter, Clar specifically referred to working in the States of Vermont and Massachusetts during this period of his life.

Throughout the latter part of 1848 isolated and generally disregarded stories of the California gold strike reached the Eastern States. But when President Polk in December officially acknowledged its probable importance and certain existence, the trek of the Argonauts began, each with his declared intent of coming back with gold whether or not he actually understood the true and varied impelling reasons for his going.

It is doubtful that John Clar was running away from something so much as returning to a land that could well have left a lingering impression upon a young seafarer. He was in the prime of life, unmarried, and probably motivated by the same spirit of striking out anew that had caused him to desert his native world in his nineteenth year. At any rate, he found himself in the Port of Panama in April of the year 1849.

This veteran of Cape Horn passage was apparently in a hurry, and had traveled the Isthmus route. He was not alone. Crowds of Americans and no small number of other nationals were trying to secure passage northward. On the Eastern Seaboard ships of every description had been converted to passenger service. Since hundreds of them failed to return because of desertion among the crews at San Francisco there was soon difficulty in obtaining sea transportation.

There are numerous recorded stories of personal trials and adventure involving the great California Gold Rush of '49; in the wagon trains overland, in ships around the Horn and from the East Pacific, in parties surviving or falling in the fever-ridden jungles of the Isthmus. It might well be claimed, however, that no single party established for itself such a clannish and devoted brotherhood as those who sailed on the *Alexander von Humboldt* from Panama to San Francisco in 1849. Probably that was because an unusual number of the passengers became prominent in California. It is also possible that the ordeal suffered by this party did indeed stand forth among the numerous annals of immigrant hardship, at least among those seekers of the Golden Fleece who, like Jason, traveled by sea.

Collis P. Huntington, and James Irvine whose name is now involved with a great university, will no doubt be recognized among the prominent passengers of the *Humboldt*. There were others no less worthy, such as J. W. Alvord, later Mayor of San Francisco, portrait painter Stephen W. Shaw, and the eminent physician Dr. John F. Morse. The latter not only assumed a prominent role in improving medical facilities and public health regulations in California; he also served as first editor of the newspaper *Sacramento Union* which was founded in 1851.

One of the passengers, James E. Gordon, came with his mother and two sisters, the only women aboard. His father was then engaged in milling redwood lumber not far from the present Santa Cruz Campus of the University of California. Gordon wrote the most complete record of the "Voyage of the Old Ship Humboldt." This account was printed in *The Pioneer* in 1898 and again in 1944 by the Society of California Pioneers. Gordon was custodian of records of the "Humboldters." This was the Alexander von

Humboldt Society which had been founded by the passengers and ship's officers.

As an indication of the togetherness of this group of pioneers, a resolution proposed by Huntington at their annual meeting of 1878 is presented in brief. This occurred precisely 29 years following that August 30th when the ship *Humboldt* dropped anchor in San Francisco Bay. It was resolved that the members "meet together each year on this day to celebrate, by a suitable banquet, the old memories attached to our voyage to this State . . . we mutually promise to set apart a chair and plate at each such occasion . . . as well after death as during their lifetime. . . . "

Also in the Gordon article is a group collection of 30 pictures of passengers including captains McArthur and Clar. These surround a ticket of passage sold by the owners of the vessel in Panama.

The story which follows will not repeat much of the detail of the long voyage. It does, however, present a few corollary incidents not heretofore gathered into the record of this particular event. And in passing, it would not be amiss to remind the reader that every researcher into historic details of that era and place all too quickly learns that most of the precious sources of reference were destroyed in the earthquake and fire of 1906.

The Isthmus region, and the present country of Columbia, in 1849 were combined as the newly independent nation of New Granada. Although travel across the Isthmus was tortuous and sickness caused many deaths, this was nevertheless a popular route from the Eastern States to California.

American business men seemed to have been well established in Panama City. Americans published the English language newspaper *Panama Star*. That journal printed advertisements and gave the general news of the day, including reports of travelers and travel conditions. News of cholera, how to keep one's health, and obituaries of the departed occupied considerable space.

The *Star* in the issue of May 13, 1849, editorialized at length about sailing ships and especially regarding the barque *Humboldt*. The article was headed "Good Time Coming." A casual reader a century and quarter later must suspect that the newspaper publisher owned a piece of *Humboldt*, or the ship's owner owned a piece of the *Star*.

The article began by telling of mistreatment of many American passengers who were paying enormous fares on overcrowded vessels. But there were now 15 or 20 vessels in port, declared the newspaper, and competition would surely improve travel conditions. Two other vessels, *Sylph* and *Niantic*, were mentioned by name.[9] Then the comforts of ship *Humboldt* were extolled. There would be "passage with all possible dispatch and on the finest scale the country will permit. She is unquestionably a splendid ship and finished in a style equal to any Livermore packet." The fine quarters for first and second class passengers were described and declared to be well-lighted and well-ventilated. Then a long list of fine foods taken aboard was presented, with the last item being "ten dozen fowls for the sick."

The 800 ton vessel had just been purchased by R. H. Leetch and Company. Berths were not yet all taken but tickets were being sold rapidly. The owners were confident *Humboldt* would be ready to sail by Saturday the 5th of May. So declared the news article.

The tonnage given for a vessel at that time, with the possible exception of warships, was a most dubious indication of size. Gordon said *Humboldt* was a Dutch barque of about 540 tons capacity. This was probably a reliable cargo estimate. He also said she was built in Bremen in 1844. Bremen was an independent German State at that time. One passenger later made the dubious statement that the ship had been a whaler, and that old whale oil barrels were used to carry the supply of drinking water. It seems more likely that the most recent use of this barque had been the transportation of a cargo of coal around the Horn to Panama in late 1848.

Conflicting recollections make it difficult to estimate the true conditions of the vessel. Gordon says the *Humboldt* was "five years old at the time . . . a very well built craft, with cabins finely finished in rosewood . . ."

The idle ship had been waiting a cargo at Panama when the firm of Ferand and Leetch saw enough profit in the impatient gold-seekers to cause them to pay an exorbitant price of $60,000 for the vessel. Gordon says they almost recovered half that investment by selling 100 more tickets to passengers than the vessel could carry. Steerage tickets were worth 100 dollars and cabin berths

---

[9]One year later the **Niantic** was a hotel on dry land in downtown San Francisco. The waterfront had been filled in behind her. See the sketch in **Mountains and Molehills** by Frank Maryat.

brought 300 dollars. Actually, as it turned out, that price acquired only one-third of a bunk in the greatly overcrowded vessel.

Said passenger Gordon: "The passengers however, did not propose to tamely submit to anything of the kind and an indignation meeting was held, the captain forbidden to hoist anchor, and the owners were made prisoner on board their own ship and not released until, on their bended knees, they had promised to charter a brig then lying in the harbor to which eighty-four of the passengers were at once transferred." This last episode was decided by lot and executed through physical force, according to Gordon.

At the same time a committee of passengers examined the food supplies and found them inadequate and of "such poor quality that much sickness and death will result from its consumption." The owners refused to improve the stores. Gordon declares the committee thereupon purchased whatever was needed with the intention upon their arrival in San Francisco of filing a lien on the vessel for their advances.

Because the vessel had not been built in the United States it could not be registered as an American vessel. So it carried the New Granadian flag. Apparently this move required a subsequent step. A New Granadian "paper captain" named José Lasso, plus 15 local crewmen went aboard. There were also 15 seamen said to be American. Crew and passengers constituted 400 in total at the start of the voyage.

W. P. McArthur, who probably was an acting ranking lieutenant of the U. S. Navy, happened to be at Panama. Why or by what authority he assumed civil command is not known. James Anthony, a passenger, later wrote, "Commander McArthur of the Navy who was in Panama on his way to San Francisco to take command of the St. Mary's was selected Captain; a happier choice could not have been made. What a genial, whole souled fellow he was!"

Presumably, Anthony was referring to the U. S. Sloop of War *St. Mary.* As a matter of fact, McArthur spent the year 1850 in charge of an official survey vessel charting the coastline from Monterey to the Columbia River. Preceding the Panama incident he had been engaged in scientific observations along the equator. In the relatively small American Navy of that time it is very probable that fellow officers McArthur and Clar had become acquainted in earlier days.

Gordon says that the command of the *Humboldt* was first offered Clar and then given to McArthur. The following letter pretty well explains the situation, except to relate that Clar actually assumed the responsibility of sailing master. This duty at least assured the proper pronunciation and also the recollection of his name for decades thereafter because some wit among the passengers declared: "Captain Clar tells us where we are."

Panama May 16th 1849

Capt J. Clar
On board the Humboldt
  Dear Sir,

Capt McArthur will tell you that we had requested him to transfer the command of the Ship Humboldt to you after his arrival in San Francisco and beg you will take charge of said Ship according to our agreement keeping Mr. McDonald as your Second.

Should Mr. Leetch be in San Francisco he will be considered as the legal agent of the Ship but should it be otherwise, you will consider yourself not only master but supercargo of the Vessel and you will act to the best of our interests. The Ship is insured from San Francisco back to Panama with liberty to call at one port on the coast, but rather should not go anywhere but return direct— for her return we depend on your efforts and exertions. We have no doubt you will use them to advantage and hope nothing shall be spared to attain that end—Amongst the Ship's papers is a contract with the sailors binding themselves to return and it would be prudent to make the foreign sailors just sign each a one [contract] that you may compell them with the laws of the country to return.

General Smith during his residence here showed us some friendship with profer of his services, and from the high opinion We have of him we have no doubt he would render you any services in his power to benefit our interests.

The New Granadian Captain Señor José Lasso is not very clever young man but he belongs to a large and very respectable family and we recommend him to your best attention in case you must be his mentor and father.

The great point of this Voyage is the return of the ship which depends much on your prudence, activity and good wishes.

In case of any accident to Captain McArthur which God forbid you will consider our letter to him as addressed to you. You have our Very best wishes and remain

Sincerely yours
I. B. Ferand
R. H. Leetch & Co.

The reference was to General Percifor F. Smith, newly appointed Major General Commanding the Pacific Military Division. As such he was superior to the Chief of the Pacific Naval

Station, Commodore Thomas ap Catesby Jones. The latter could now be returned to the west coast in respectable status. General Smith had tarried at Panama for several months where he began issuing proclamations before he always knew whereof he spoke. He arrived in San Francisco at the end of March 1849, just as the great rush to the mines was getting under way.

The gold of California was to be acquired by Americans, said General Smith, and not by the riff-raff of the world. Some people, according to historian Hittell, believed that this declaration from high led to the depredations of the notorious San Francisco hoodlums known as the Hounds. This gang preyed almost exclusively upon foreigners until mid-July of 1849 when a select committee of substantial citizens brought them to trial and banishment.

There was little in the way of formal government in San Francisco. To a certain extent Smith can be charged with some blame here also. He had refused to endorse the establishment of a "district legislature" for San Francisco County, as voted by the residents in their desperate desire for something better than the interim military government. However, by the time of the arrival of the ship *Humboldt* a responsible system of courts was in operation.

Probably General Smith did most to estrange himself from the merchants and boosters of San Francisco by declaring the place could never become a commercial center because of its miserable weather, impossible dockage, and vulnerability to military attack. He established Benicia Arsenal and practically commanded that the principal city be built there.

As for the miners, the very first Legislature recognized that they were present and taxable. A law was enacted which provided that a license to mine must be obtained by any person "who is not a native of or natural born citizen under the treaty of Guadalupe Hidalgo (all native California Indians excepted)."

In the treaty of Guadalupe Hidalgo, which was concluded by representatives of the United States and Mexico at the place of that name in February of 1848, Upper California and part of the adjoining Southwest became American. Native residents automatically received United States citizenship. Indians, however, were undoubtedly regarded as wards of the Central Government.

The first California foreign miner's license fee was 20 dollars monthly. This was eventually adjusted to a monthly tax of four dollars. Throughout its legal life this type of license was valid for only one month. It required continuous renewal. As a matter of fact, since the operation of State and local government was dependent principally upon this and local property taxation for support, the Foreign Miner's Tax became an important source of income.

In San Francisco during the Gold Rush the prominent brokers and shippers Simmons, Hutchinson and Company were known as the agents or consignees of Leetch and Company of Panama. Leetch was a shipmaster himself and could have intended to arrive in San Francisco before *Humboldt*. At any rate, the *Panama Star* declared that passengers leaving on *Humboldt* must be aboard and ready to embark by the first tide of Monday [sic] May 20, 1849. Passengers had been on board since the 13th, said Gordon.[10]

On the 21st the anchor was raised, sails set, the American flag hoisted, and three cheers given for the captain, the crew, and "our wives, little ones and sweethearts at home. . . . Many a tear glistened in eyes not given to weeping among the Argonauts. . . . "

This was a lovely scene of departure for a new life in California. Unfortunately, the *Humboldt* lay becalmed off the bay of Panama for the following two weeks. Came times of pleasant weather, and also rainy weather. The passengers quarreled among themselves, arranged impromptu entertainment, and became concerned about decreasing water and food.

The mentioned A. M. Kenady was one of the passengers, aged 24 years. Twenty-five years later he recalled in respect to John Clar that "in his relating to a coterie of passengers his adventures

---

[10]May 21, 1849, was a Monday. The error in **Panama Star** could have caused confusion for years thereafter as to the time consumed in the trip to San Francisco. Two letters to Clar regarding command of **Humboldt** are in Soc. Cal. Pioneers file.

**New York Herald** in May and June of 1849 in reporting sale of **Humboldt** said it formerly sailed out of Baltimore and was "an old ship" sold "at a handsome price." On August 13, the **Herald** quoted a July letter from Panama which said, "the person who went in command knew nothing of the coast. She will not reach San Francisco until August or September." The last sentence was precisely accurate, but the first was ludicrous. McArthur and Clar together were probably unequaled in their detailed knowledge of these waters. Officially, of course, Lasso was in command.

A reminiscence assumed to have been written by James Anthony, later editor of **Sacramento Union**, is deposited at Cal. State Library. In part, he wrote: "When the writer arrived at Panama (April 3) there were only two vessels in port — the **Humboldt** and the **"Two Friends."** It was his misfortune to engage passage in the former. The vessel was chartered by three "enterprising" and unscrupulous chaps from old John B. Ferand to whom she was consigned."

Passenger and later Sacramento dentist, William W. Light, said **Humboldt** had been a whaler (Sac. **Record-Union**, Aug. 26, 1901). He also claimed they lived on jerked beef and hard tack. James Gordon details a spartan weekly menu which is somewhat better.

by land and by sea there was no more attentive listener than myself."

One thing may be assumed about the erstwhile professor and sailing master. If he knew where he was at all times he probably didn't like it. As the ship edged westerly some 600 miles waiting for a wind that would advance its northwesterly course, there was a question as to whether they should try for the Sandwich Isles or Mazatlán or Acapulco.

On May 28 the first death occurred and the burial at sea was carried out immediately. Food was poor and the water tasted as though it came from the bilge. So much bean soup was served that, according to the author Gordon, the annual banquets of the Humboldt Society in later years would have been considered a failure without that delicacy on the menu.

A hospital was constructed on deck for the ailing. On June 5th a victim of tuberculosis died, and on the 13th another succumbed. Because of the tropical climate a sea burial promptly followed each death.

It is not the nature of adventuresome immigrants to be weak in body or spirit. And this group was attended by three qualified doctors among the passengers. Dr. John F. Morse no doubt built much of the foundation here for his later distinguished career as a citizen of California.

On June 19th and July 3rd deaths occurred. The wrapped corpses were slid off a gang plank with services being conducted by the Reverend Mr. Ashby.

Came the Fourth of July and still the calms and adverse winds prevailed. Guns were fired, flags hoisted, speeches made. A banquet of fried doughnuts and ginger beer was served. Spirits revived a bit, especially when it was announced that the ship would make for Acapulco to reprovision.

*Humboldt* entered that harbor on the afternoon of August 6th and was welcomed by a very severe earthquake ashore. The Argonauts had advanced about 1700 of the 4000 miles of this sea leg of their journey. They remained for a generally pleasant ten days in the city. A subscription of money was used to acquire provisions for the remaining voyage. On August 10th another passenger died and was buried ashore. Two passengers decided to secure steamboat passage rather than further risk the good ship *Humboldt*. Two stowaways tried to take their place but were rowed back to Acapulco after the ship was well under way.

Then followed two final weeks of monotonous slow progress. On August 27 the seventh and last of the passengers to die was buried at sea. Quarrels were frequent. The food and water became poorer and more limited in quantity. On the day of the last funeral at sea a petition was being circulated among passengers which proposed confiscation of the vessel because of the miserable experience and expense they had all suffered.

But the Golden Gate was known to be near. On the 29th a brig out of San Francisco was spoken. It proved to have aboard the official delegates to the State Constitutional Convention being held at Monterey.

At noon on August 30th, Barque *Alexander von Humboldt* passed through the Golden Gate and dropped anchor near the Sloop of War *Warren*. One hundred and one days had passed since the cheerful attempt to depart from the Bay of Panama. When a representative of Simmons and Hutchinson requested Captain McArthur to move closer to shore he refused, according to Gordon.

"Three cheers were given for the captain, and Dr. Morse offered a series of resolutions thanking the officers and exonerating them from all blame in the matter. The consignees not responding, the passengers' baggage was detained and the captain ordered the vessel sold to pay her debts. On Saturday morning, September 1st, 1849, we all went ashore, our boat landing on the corner of Montgomery and Washington streets. . . . "

Dr. Morse had something to say about the arrival in a letter which he promptly mailed to his mother in Vermont. Unfortunately, he did not comment upon the disposition of the ship or the recovery of personal claims. He closed the long letter, which had been started more than a month earlier on shipboard, with these words:[11]

> Reports here had our vessel shipwrecked, cast away, the hands dead with the cholera and a variety of such inconveniences. 50 cents apiece for washing a shirt, $1 for pantaloons, about $50

[11]Letter, Dr. John F. Morse to Hannah Curtiss Morse, Bolton, Vermont, dated "Ship Humboldt July 29/49," is in Cal. State Library.

Much further illness was anticipated on the ship, wrote Morse. Eight passengers were "almost in the embrace of Old Mortality." In the end the young doctor believed his vigorous leadership in scraping and scrubbing in the steerage changed the morbid conditions and saved lives. He noted that 300 passengers were in steerage.

Apparently soon after leaving Acapulco he wrote, "We are now making tolerable time and if we should be continously fortunate we may be in S. Francisco in the course of 3 weeks from the foregoing date. But the Ax Humboldt is a miserable per week at the best Hotels for Board, eggs 50 cents apiece and to great reluctance upon the part of the Hens to lay them at that,— milk $1 a quart, potatoes from 25 to 50 cts per pound, onions 37 ½ cents apiece Etc. Etc. Etc.

Ever & Forever
Your affectionate Son, J. F. Morse

The changes wrought during the mere half-dozen years since his last view of the village at Yerba Buena Cove must have been startling indeed to Captain John Clar. Ashore were at least five thousand people in various conditions of residence. He was now 36 years of age. Regardless of his expectations he had become an active participant in one of the world's most frenzied adventures.

His immediate occupation seems to have been well planned for him, even though its execution promptly faltered. On September 10th some official of Simmons, Hutchinson and Company scrawled his illegible signature on a letter which said:

We wish you to retain the command of the Ship Alex Von Humboldt until we relieve you by a substitute. We also wish Mr. McDonald to continue as mate for the present.

Yours respectfully

The trail of John Clar is dim for almost two years following that letter and considerable research fails to reveal the precise fate of the *Humboldt*, or settle the question of claims presented by the passengers. As late as mid-November the ship was listed as an arrival in port with Lasso in Command.

At the time of Clar's death the San Francisco *Morning Call* printed a five inch obituary column in which the *Humboldt* voyage was featured. Prominent local surviving passengers were named. And it was declared: "The old ship was condemned on her arrival at San Francisco, and sold for $12,000." This was only 34 years after the event. However, the newspaper advertisement described ahead casts considerable doubt upon the accuracy of that statement.

Historian Bancroft says, "By the middle of November [of 1849] upward to 600 vessels had entered the harbor, and in the following year came still more. The larger proportion were left to swing at anchor in the bay, almost without guard."

In September of 1850 a list was made by name of 660 sea-going vessels in San Francisco Bay.[12] It was not indicated how

---

sailor." This last comment, by a Vermont landlubber, is the only firm statement this writer has discovered about the sailing qualities of this barque-rigged vessel.

The unpredictability of voyages under sail is indicated by this record of 1849 runs from Panama to San Francisco; *Niantic* 68 days; *Sylph* 76; *Two Friends* 165. The steamships required 20 to 23 days.

[12]**Pac. Marine Review.**

many were engaged in scheduled runs out of the Bay. Some of the idle vessels near shore were utilized as living quarters and one was an official prison ship.

Government control was attempted from military headquarters at Monterey. Alta California was commonly referred to as a territory of the United States in that period. During 1850 the county courts of session were initiated. They preceded the county boards of supervisors. Elections for local offices were held. And the alcalde court system of justice was not being accepted graciously by the motley, migratory immigrants of practially all nations, General Percifor Smith notwithstanding.

It has been estimated, and probably conservatively, that 3000 men of the new population explosion had recently been regular hands on the various ships that had entered San Francisco Bay. The newspaper *Alta California* carried a repeated advertisement over the signature of Commodore Thomas ap Catesby Jones who had returned as Chief of the Pacific Station. He declared that deserters from the United States Navy would learn of his forgiving nature if they would return to duty.

Then on December 24 and 26 of 1849 the *Alta* carried this brief advertisement:

> ...sailing, clipper built brig MATADOR, Capt. J. Wesch, will leave for the above named port on the 1st day of January next. For freight or passage apply to
> 7-2*　　　　　　　　　　　　WARD & CO.
>
> The Ship HUMBOLDT, 849 tons register, three and a half years old, is offered for sale on favorable terms.
> 7　　　　SIMMONS, HUTCHINSON & CO.
>
> FOR VALPARAISO, Direct.—The A 1, ship PACIFIC to sail positively on 1st Janua-

Very likely both American and New Granadian crew members had long since headed for the gold diggings. It is quite certain that Captain Clar did not take *Humboldt* or any other vessel back on the Panama run. In fact, it is doubtful if he associated further with ocean transportation except as a passenger. Perhaps, as vague family anecdote indicates, he did engage in the business of transporting fresh water from the Sausalito side for sale to vessels anchored off San Francisco. This was a thoroughly solid business venture of the time.

The determination of the fate of the "good ship *Humboldt*" became a challenge out of all proportion to its importance in this writing. The available evidence leads one to suspect that the demand for reimbursement on the part of the passengers has been inaccurately construed in later years to have been a condemnation of the ship for unseaworthiness. Also, the well known difficulty of making northwesterly progress in those waters has been charged in this case to both inefficiency on the part of the ship's command and the poor sailing quality of the vessel. No valid evidence supports either charge.

Clearly, it was impossible in 1849 to obtain a crew in San Francisco. So, the *Humboldt* either joined the other hundreds of abandoned hulks which eventually sank into the bottom mud, or she was cannibalized for shore construction. Or possibly she was purchased in the last days of 1849 with no surviving record of that transaction. The fact that this ship was not an American flag vessel eliminates a prime informational source in Customs Department official records.

In regard to the collection of claims by the passengers, it is probable that the system of responsible courts established after August 1st, 1849, in San Francisco would have adequately handled such a case. Unfortunately, such records were lost in the fire of 1906.

If the legendary Judge William B. Almond was on the bench it is probable that the consignees settled out of court, and promptly. We do know that in December a special court of first instance was created to consider civil matters and that Almond was appointed to sit in this court. This he is alleged to have done in red miner's shirt, boots on the fireplace mantle, whittling on his fingernails whilst handing down decisions without benefit of counsel and with a minimum of testimony presented.

His Honor seems to have felt the presence of lawyers in court was a waste of precious time if they were allowed to interfere, and especially if they represented ship masters or owners. Historian Hittell (vol 2, 779) tells of an attorney who was at least allowed to read a pertinent passage from Blackstone after Judge Almond had already heard the case to his own satisfaction and had rendered a final decision. Told that more conversation would be of no avail the lawyer replied, "I am aware of that, but I am simply reading this passage to show you what an old fool Blackstone was."

One interesting item in regard to the ship *Humboldt* remains. At the annual meeting of the Alexander von Humboldt Society held on August 30, 1864, the following news note has been preserved.

"At the meeting a letter was read from sailing master Clar, whom sickness detained, transmitting the log book of the A. Von Humboldt. This interesting and valuable document was recently found among a lot of rubbish and presented to this anniversary gathering. . . . "

Unquestionably, the log was destroyed in 1906. It would be interesting to know how Clar came into its possession in 1864. It would also be interesting to know to what extent the business ethics of the ship owners, as evidenced in the voyage of 1849, affected this young captain's refusal to accept his first important command.

# 6 And There Was the Land

The activities of John Clar after June of 1851 are set forth principally in the records of land acquisition and land surveying. To have been so heavily involved then it must be assumed that in the prior months he had been very busy in the profession he knew well and which he unquestionably performed honorably, that is, land surveying.

Many of the serious Argonauts knew well that the wealth of California would not continue to exist in the chance drift of gold quartz veins or ancient stream beds, but rather in the obvious agricultural and industrial opportunities of a growing community.

Some of the newcomers substituted deceit, fraud and boldness for common business integrity. Historian Bancroft never hesitated to call a scoundrel by his proper name. In respect to the California land situation of this era he wrote:

"A kind of moral intoxication, a gold-drunkenness, had debased the public mind and distorted spiritual vision, until men esteemed it a distinction to become noted for procuring or handling, even for stealing, large sums of money; and it was only when their own fortunes, or lives, were in danger, that their fellows plucked up enough courage to rebuke them."

John Clar saw the opportunities around him and he made the best effort within his means to acquire two valuable properties. The first and most important concerns the story of the Encinal de Temescal, now called Oakland. Because several interrelated actions were occurring approximately simultaneously during a three or four year period, it is believed the Oakland incident will be followed most easily if it is told separately. And the telling will be confined to that aspect of the complex land muddle as it bore upon the principal subject of this writing.

It is necessary to understand the general conditions of land ownership during this hectic period. The United States had taken by military conquest a rather indefinite and vaguely known, but certainly huge body of land commonly known as Alta or Upper

California. From mid-1846 until statehood was granted by Congress in September of 1850, government control must have been exceedingly nebulous where it existed at all. And the State government which practically inserted itself into the situation in the last days of 1849 was faced with huge organizational and operational problems that probably would have overwhelmed any less energetic and determined populace. One of the first problems was to describe the new State geographically, and then later to delineate its boundaries.

One principle was held to be right and valid. Such land as had come into the actual possession of any person by grant of Spain or Mexico or by purchase was the owner's to have and to hold under the new government. Under the prevailing conditions the national government performed a fairly creditable job in trying to redeem this promise to the old residents. This was not easy.

Some early acquisitions and claimed acquisitions of land were fraudulent. Others were involved in family quarrels. In most cases the size and location of the claimed land was vague.

There had been plenty of land, and a few hundred acres more or less were of little concern. Land grants were bounded by streams or lines extending from a tree to a mountain top, extending in distance an assumed number of *varas*. This Spanish unit of measure will be discussed in detail later.

Such land as was not situated in a recognized grant, or in a pueblo, presidio, or remnant of the old mission holdings had automatically become the American public domain just as it had first been Spanish crown land, and then Mexican public domain.

Presumably a terribly mixed-up situation could have become worse had not the hectic scrambling for gold occurred almost entirely upon the public domain rather than upon private property. Gold seekers would certainly have disregarded all commonly accepted private rights other than their own self-imposed rules of local conduct. The actions, sometimes violent and vindictive, of squatters and trespassers elsewhere than in the gold region bears ample evidence of the temper of many of the immigrants.

In 1851 two very important California offices of the Federal (more commonly called Central or General) Government were established in San Francisco. These offices were closely related to each other within the Department of Interior. One was the Office of United States Surveyor-General, usually referred to as the Land Office. The other was the United States Land Claims

Commission (sometimes referred to as the Board of Land Commissioners). Incidentally, at the same period an office of State Surveyor-General was established in Sacramento, principally to handle those public lands transferred to the State of California.

The Land Office in San Francisco began its work in June of 1851 under Samuel D. King. By December of that year the Land Claims Commission, consisting of three presidential appointees, was ready to begin its labors.

The single duty of the Commission was to hear and act upon the validity of all Spanish or Mexican grants of land in pre-American California. This was a vitally serious task. Under the intense pressures of the day, the Commissioners (generally called "judges") must be credited with having done a satisfactory job on their individual parts. Some greedy private attorneys are not so happily remembered.

In essence it might be said that the U. S. Government was challenging the grant holders to prove their individual claims as the proper persons upon the properly described lands. Losers in any Commission determination were privileged to appeal the decision before a District Federal Court or the Supreme Court. At that period California was served by a Northern and a Southern District Court. Their areas of jurisdiction met at the approximate location of present Fresno.

The creation of the Land Claims Commission by Congress was essentially the work of California's Senator William M. Gwin. That gentleman was an immigrant from the Southern States, and eventually he deserted the Union cause. Prior to that time, however, it would be proper to remember that he led in sponsoring the establishment of the Pony Express as a communication link binding the Golden State to the troubled Central Government on the East Coast on the eve of civil war. In respect to the creation of the Land Claims Commission, it seems clear that Gwin's personal sympathies lay with the land-hungry American immigrants.

The Commission was permitted under law to hire one secretary and no more than five clerks. In this case the term clerk referred to qualified technical assistants. The clerks were compensated at a salary of $1500 per year for their services.

The U. S. Surveyor-General assumed the duty of surveying and mapping the State outside the delineated land grants. He also recorded the disposition of parcels of public lands to the various parties acquiring them. The Spanish system of land subdivision, as already indicated, was by metes and bounds, that is, from point to point in any direction.

After due consideration, the Americans departed from this system of land identification. The township system of square units arbitrarily criss-crossing the landscape was adopted. This system of square mile subdivisions was more easily applied to the mid-west prairies than to mountainous terrain. Surveyor-General King raised the question of adequacy of this system in California. Nevertheless, by September of 1851 a survey party under Colonel Leander Ransome was already in the field running lines east and west and north and south of the selected master control point, the summit of Mt. Diablo.

John Clar served as a valuable employee, first with the Land Claims Commission and then with the Surveyor-General. The two offices were closely inter-related. When he went from one to the other is not precisely clear. As a matter of fact, a couple of other things were happening to him at the same time, as has been inferred.

The next documented record of John Clar's whereabouts following the arrival of ship *Humboldt* places him across the Golden Gate in the Year of our Lord 1851; and of California Statehood, nine months through Year One. He had completed a map of the proposed village of Sausalito by early June of 1851. Probably the map no longer exists. However, the Marin County Historical Society possesses an 1853 assessment roll which indicates that the prominent attorney and publisher Charles T. Botts, then a resident of San Francisco, acquired the entire area. The assessor declared that town lots and their ownership in 1853 were indicated on "the map drawn and surveyed of Sausalito by John Clar, June 8, 1851."

This map is referred to in another case in the first book of Marin County deeds, as does the notation that Clar appeared as a witness on a land transaction in that county on April 24, 1852.

Shortly after election day, September 17, 1851, one Ai Barney, Deputy County Clerk, addressed an undated letter to J. Clar which states:

Sir

I do hereby certify that you have received the highest number of votes polled at the General Election on the third Wednesday of September A.D. 1851 for the Office of County Surveyor of the said County of Marin, are duly elected to that office for the term prescribed by law.

No record of votes cast is available. There could hardly have been many more than one hundred since the population of the county was about a thousand. That included more than 200 Indians, the non-voting women, and the usual legions of *Californio* children.

According to the Statutes of 1850 a County Surveyor appeared to have a near monopoly in his own territory. In fact, if he declined to perform any survey "upon application of any individual or corporation" or as required by the Court of Sessions he could be fined up to $200. No salary was stipulated, but the law provided a standard list of fees for surveying services. Earliest annual reports of the State Surveyor-General include expressions of dissatisfaction from the County Surveyors regarding insufficient income, difficult terrain and harrassment by Indians.

This particular activity in John Clar's life seems to have been forgotten in family anecdotes. Possibily it was considered unimportant. Yet this writer does remember his father saying, "My father said that during one day in Marin County he ran across eighteen grizzly bear."

The records of the Court of Sessions of the County of Marin on the 8th day of September, 1852, declared that the sheriff shall be appointed collector of taxes; and, further,

> Whereas John Clar the County Surveyor of this County has ceased
> to be a resident of this County and the Office of County Surveyor
> has become vacant . . . it is ordered that the vacancy be filled by the
> appointment of B. F. Carter . . .

One month after Clar assumed the county surveyor position in 1851 he signed a contract to purchase the Encinal on the other side of the Bay. Less than three months after that he was hired by the Land Claims Commission.

From the Commission office in San Francisco he received a letter dated December 22, 1851. It was signed by two of the commissioners or judges, Hiland Hall and James Wilson. The letter said:

> In consequence of the trust and confidence reposed in you by the
> Commissioners for ascertaining and settling private land claims
> in the State of California, they have appointed you a clerk to said
> Commission to hold the office during the pleasure of the board.

At this time the few newspapers began devoting several columns to the lengthy instructions pertaining to the adjudication of land titles as set forth by the Board of Land Commissioners.

In July of 1852 the State of California conducted the only regular citizen census ever taken by the State. The reason is said to have originated in the dubious quality of the federal census of 1850. At any rate, in the San Francisco record appears the name John Clar; occupation "clerk", resident of Virginia and native of Spain. The point of interest is the association of that name with the preceding entry. This is simply "H. L. Thornton, Land Commission." That gentleman was indeed one of the three judges serving under presidential appointment.

Records of court cases of land adjudication often show the name of John Clar as a technical witness. Sometimes there were other better known names in association, such as that of John Sutter.

Then on August 10th of 1852 the respected clerk addressed a letter to his employers, the Commissioners, advising them that he could not move south in their continued employ. Obviously, land claimants in the Southern District were now to receive the attention of this court. John said he could not go because of "circumstances of an insuperable nature." Nevertheless, he was most anxious to serve the board in any capacity that he could.

The circumstances holding him in the Bay area must certainly have been the growing complexities involved with the Oakland purchase. This man had no local home ties and the work of the commission suited him ideally.

In the Kenady letter of thirty years later he had something to say of that particular work. The following quotation should be read with an appreciation of the letter's basic intent. The author was listing his technical qualifications for employment.

> Amidst a multiplicity of duties I gave the elements for the map of California, showed how to segregate private from public lands, and so forth. In the latter years I have copied and translated the one thousand cases of original land claims in the office and those presented to the Land Commission. The Spanish Archives, from the vicissitudes of time and removal to and from adobe buildings, have become, in cases of land claims, dilapidated and illegible, and also from constant use of them in courts. These I have deciphered without missing a syllable and have collated the various documents so as to give a full history of each case. I have recorded this work in 23 large volumes of 700 pages each, and 2 larger volumes of original maps.

Whether the so-called Spanish Archives of the State Archives in Sacramento are the essential result of the long and tedious task described above is not precisely known. This writer had reasonable assurance from a handwriting expert that they were. On the other hand, the Land Office records in San Francisco in 1906 were partially destroyed by fire.

In October of 1852, Clar moved over to Surveyor-General King's office. His title was still clerk and he received the substantial salary of $183 monthly.

In March of the following year, one of California's most interesting characters succeeded Mr. King. This was John Coffee Hays, commonly referred to by his friends as "the Colonel" and by intimates as Jack.[13]

At this time Hays had been performing a creditable job as Sheriff of San Francisco County which then included present San Mateo County. Hays was internationally known for his early reputation as a classic Western law-man. At age 23, he had been a captain of Texas Rangers. As an indication of that reputation it later happened that this native of Kentucky sat out the Civil War in his Oakland home after refusing a general's commission offered by both Union and Confederacy.

John Clar had some firm business dealings with Jack Hays more than a year before the latter became Surveyor-General. This will be made evident in the history of the Oakland purchase.

In the Land Office after the arrival of Hays, Clar's salary was raised to 208 dollars monthly. In a deposition as a witness in a land case of December 1853, he testified that he was Keeper of the Spanish and Mexican Archives in the Office of Surveyor-General and had charge of surveys of private claims. He was also officially termed Translator. This employment continued until the fall of 1857.

The squatter issue was of paramount political and economic importance at this time. The United States Government maintained that all valid land titles obtained under Spanish and Mexican laws must be honored. Hordes of immigrants wanted land and they insisted that it was not morally proper for single owners to control vast blocks of land especially now that their own government was in control by right of conquest. Evidence in the form of homestead and water laws indicates that both the Federal and the State governments officially favored, and presumably still favor,

---

[13]See **Colonel Jack Hays,** by J.K. Greer (1952).

land settlement in which the many rather than the few are in right of possession of the land.

California officials persistently pressed the Central Government to transfer complete jurisdiction and control of the entire public domain to California. This plea can be found in repeated legislative resolutions and gubernatorial messages of the period. As the pressure of voting immigrants became heavier the tendency to appease them quite naturally grew in the State Legislature. The Settler's Protection Act of 1856 and the reaction it brought will be discussed later to illustrate the extent of the seemingly inevitable confrontation.

John Clar viewed this great drama of land occupation during the vital first decades of American California history from a vantage point enjoyed by few other observers. Not only was he a professional witness; he was a vitally active participant in two particular cases. And further, the considerable technical diversity of the two cases, and his respective interest in each, make them ideal historical examples of the range of conditions inherent in these bitter struggles. Therefore, the general legal, political and economic situation surrounding the struggle of men to possess and hold the land of the Mexican ranchos called San Antonio and Tzábaco will be explored in the two chapters which follow.

Unfortunately, this man left too little memoranda regarding either his activities or his later personal reflections upon the land occupation experience. This writer's father used to say, "My father used to say that things had to change rapidly in California when the Americans came. He was never bitter about what happened."

Yet this writer also remembers that few subjects seemed to agitate his father so much as talk of property quarrels. Without question, in his infancy and childhood this man had heard numerous discussions and possibly quarrels about land ownership involving his father both as claimant and as technical witness. In fact, on the day of his birth, this child's mother was the owner of record of a homestead land parcel which failed to maintain its validity in law.

However, it is best to move back in time some seven years to the fall of 1851. Consider now the prevailing situation across the bay from San Francisco, on the *contra costa*.

*First the Golden Age, and then the Age of Gold.*
*How different! And yet between the end and the*
*beginning of a decade California gives us a specimen*
*of each, which brief period presents two episodes of*
*society the history of the world cannot parallel. Both*
*were original, both phenomenal; and so closely upon*
*the heels of one followed another, that for an instant*
*both were on the ground at the same time.*

*It was when the gold-seekers came that this golden*
*age of California was destined to be alloyed with brass;*
*for not the age of gold was California's true golden*
*age. The age of gold was the age of avarice . . . .*
*More nearly resembling the euthanasia of the ancients*
*was the pastoral life preceding the finding of the*
*Sierra treasures.*

H. H. Bancroft
*California Pastoral*

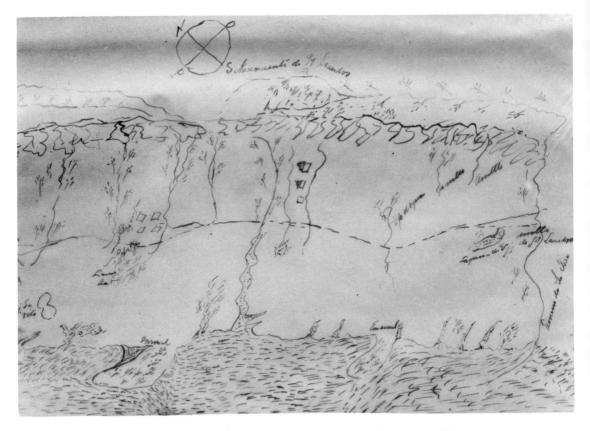

## DISEÑO OF RANCHO SAN ANTONIO OF LUIS PERALTA

In 1820 when Solá was Spanish Colonial Governor of California, old soldier Luis Peralta received a grant of land which is presently most often referred to as The East Bay Area. The original application and other papers were lost. This rough sketch or **diseño** of the grant was made in 1844.

The southwest side is obviously San Francisco Bay, or "the sea" as quoted in the written rancho description. On the northeast side, the summit of what is presently called the Berkeley Hills forms the boundary.

On the north, or northwest side a boundary stream flows directly into the bay. It was described as the Arroyo de Los Cerritos de San Antonio. Near the mouth of this arroyo a crude "Se-rita" and the figure-eight loop on the **diseño** indicate the prominent Little Hill, or El Cerrito de San Antonio, at the present boundary of Alameda and Contra Costa counties.

Ownership of land across the arroyo on the south side is shown to be **Terreno de los Peraltas.**

At the upper left of the **diseño,** over the summit, there is an indication of presently named Wildcat Creek flowing northwest. And to the right, southeasterly, is the birthland, or **nacimiento,** of San Leandro Creek. The Arroyo de San Leandro becomes the southeast and south boundary of the Peralta grant, separating it from the "Terreno de San Jose." (Actually, the latter area became an Estudillo grant).

A road courses through the property. This was the Camino of Rancho San Antonio. From Lake Merritt southward it generally paralleled the present MacArthur Freeway. A few squares drawn at two places undoubtedly represent the home ranches of a couple of the four sons of Luis Peralta. It is probable that the more northerly structures represent the buildings of Vicente on Temescal Creek, and those at the center of the sketch are the Antonio Peralta ranch buildings.

At two places near the road are indicated an **ojo de agua,** which is a flowing spring. For the **rancheros** these must have been landmarks of high importance. Along the bay shore a wide intrusion surely was intended to represent the Creek or Estuary of San Antonio, which is present day Oakland Inner Harbor. On either side are peninsulas, each clearly marked Encinal, or "oak grove." The northernmost must have been the Encinal de Temescal which became downtown Oakland. The southern was Encinal de Bolsa or later Alameda.

# 7 The Encinal Called Oakland

Luis Peralta was only a boy when he journeyed to Alta California with the Anza party in 1776. Later he joined the colonial army. In 1820 he asked for a grant of land from Spanish Governor Pablo Vicente de Sola. A couple of years thereafter the grant was approved. It embraced the entire East Bay area from present Richmond City to San Leandro. In 1842 old Don Luis divided this San Antonio Rancho among his four sons.

Son Vicente occupied what was generally called Temescal. It extended from San Antonio Creek in present East Oakland north into Berkeley. His *hacienda* headquarters were situated just north of the present junction of Telegraph and Claremont avenues.

Vicente has been described as of rather light complexion, "handsome, six feet tall, weighing 225 pounds, straight as an arrow, hospitable, kind and full of native dignity." His charming wife was the former Señorita Encarnación Galindo, whose family owned the Laguna de la Merced Rancho which constituted the northwestern part of San Francisco Peninsula.

The East Bay flatlands, rising gently to the base of the steep eastern hills, had for years been the open pastures of Peralta cattle. Hides and tallow were practically the only product of the land until the oakwood fuel and redwood timber in the back canyon began to be harvested by the increasing *Anglo* population. John Sutter used to send boats and crews down-river from New Helvetia to split and whipsaw lumber in "Peralta's red woods."

A specialist in cultural geography prior to the Gold Rush would probably have declared that the most important business and population center of the San Francisco region would develop on the broad flats of the eastern shore. A logical site would have been where the great rivers of the interior entered the bay. In fact, several prominent business men of the time were certain that Benicia would become the queen city. Instead, however, the isolated San Francisco Peninsula soon outstripped the East Bay in population and industrial importance. The east side became known as the *contra costa*, or "opposite coast." No doubt, the mud flats and sand bars along the eastern shore were an important factor in discouraging water borne commerce.

The area that now constitutes downtown Oakland City was apparently regarded by Vicente Peralta as a peninsula. This was because one arm of the Estero Antonio (Oakland Inner Harbor) hooked up, to the north. Presently this water intrusion is called Lake Merritt.

On this peninsula the coast live oak, called *encina*, grew in great profusion. Indians had apparently built sweathouses here. So the area was commonly called Encinal de Temescal, the "oakgrove by the sweathouses." It will be noted later, however, that in one formal description of the area another version of that name was recorded. This was the term Ensinar.

Even before the Gold Rush a number of people were becoming interested in acquiring property on the Temescal or Encinal flats. Several must have negotiated small leases with Peralta. At any rate, it will become apparent that a few were occupying property with his knowledge and consent. Then, with the tremendous immigration of fortune seekers, hundreds of squatters came and settled upon the land. Most of them were determined to stay regardless of the legality of such behavior. The first East Bay squatter is said to have taken root there in the winter of 1849-50.

The story of the acquisition of property on the East Bay flats is very complicated. For 30 years following the arrival of the first squatters many land titles were under some legal cloud; and there were ponderous contests brought before the courts.

This writing will attempt simply to discuss the initial conditions of the transfer of land in the Encinal from Vicente Peralta to others. The time period of particular interest may be limited essentially to the years 1850 through 1854. However, even such a superficial treatment is complicated by the fact that three primary parties were involved in trying to acquire the Encinal at the same time.

These primary parties were: William Heath Davis and associates; the Carpentier-Adams-Moon faction; John Clar and associates. They will be dealt with in that order. However, because much of the activity of the several parties occurred concurrently, three of the most critical events are noted below with their dates in chronological order. It seems logical that Peralta's relationship with, or response to each of the parties must have been affected by the particular approach of each party of interest as it occurred. The three critical events were as follows. On October 3, 1851, a contract of sale from Peralta to John Clar was recorded; on March

13, 1852, a formal sale to Clar and associates was made; on May 4, 1852, a town of Oakland was created by State statute.

First, there was the old pioneer William Heath Davis who, as a youth, had come to Monterey and then San Francisco to work for his uncle, the merchant Nathan Spear. Davis had been sent to the Encinal as early as 1840 to buy hides and tallow. The young man greatly admired Don Vicente and the charming Señora Encarnación. Davis declared that in 1846 and again in 1850 he tried to persuade Peralta to sell him two-thirds of (or interest in) the Encinal de Temescal.

It is quite possible that the order of events during the course of these fantastic early years may have been confused in their recitation by the respected Davis when he wrote his story in the last years of his long life. At any rate, Davis represented a company of active citizens of San Francisco who came to Peralta with a proposition for the orderly settlement of the Oakland area as a borough of San Francisco.

In his book, Davis mentioned 16 names of prominent San Franciscans of that era and declared there were many others who wished to purchase "a block or more of land for a retreat so near the metropolis." Among the personages named were Sam Brannan, Alcalde George Hyde, William Leidesdorff, Robert Ridley, Francisco Guerrero and Josiah Belden. Davis said he informed Peralta that these "best and wealthiest people of San Francisco would be a bodyguard against the appropiation without his knowledge and consent." This was a questionable assurance in view of the mass pressure of squatters at that time and place.

Davis declared that he offered Peralta the sum of $5,000, plus a share of the income from future sales of lots. His party would also build a church and a wharf and operate a ferry boat to San Francisco. This occurred in 1849, he says, although it surely must have been nearer 1850.

Said Davis, "In the forepart of 1850 I made my last call on Don Vicente on this business, to renew once more my offer. At this time the Encinal de Temescal was covered with squatters. But I received the same reply as before."

It will be remembered that when Commodore Jones brought his little squadron into Monterey Bay in 1842 they first captured a Mexican barque. Señorita Estudillo had been on that ship and consequently was made a prisoner of war for a few hours. Later, as a member of the Bay community, the young lady attended the gay parties hosted by Commodore Jones while the *Cyane* was anchored off Sausalito. The señorita was a niece of the wife of Captain Richardson of San Rafael.

Davis was there, and both he and Gunner Meyers mentioned the affairs in their writings. It seems reasonable to assume that during one or more of these events the young professor with the fluent Spanish tongue, the continental manners, the dark and liquid eyes, became acquainted with the future Mrs. William H. Davis.

What part Mrs. Davis played in her husband's conflict of interest with John Clar eight years after the gay parties is quite unknown. But another pair of "daughters of the country," sisters in fact, were evident in the close background of the Contra Costa incident. The reader is asked to note this last aspect of the Davis-Peralta negotiation because its sequel is believed to appear quite oddly a full 30 years later.

It is necessary at this point to introduce a particular friend of Davis, the prominent James Alexander Forbes, Sr. who had come to California about 1830 and had been the British Consul. He had married one of the Galindo maidens, thus becoming a brother-in-law of Señora Vicente Peralta. Davis declared that Forbes came to Encinal de Temescal to urge Don Vicente to sell the major share of the Encinal as proposed by Davis. In spite of this persuasion, Peralta was unwilling. And Davis noted in his book that years later the old Don met him in downtown Oakland and admitted the error of his earlier decision. That conclusion is, of course, presented as hindsight by one unsuccessful party of interest.

Peralta had reason to be concerned about squatters when Davis made his last proposal to purchase the Encinal. On May 16, 1850, Edson Adams set out a claim of 160 acres at the present foot of Broadway under the presumption that he was on the public domain. Then Andrew J. Moon and Horace W. Carpentier came and did likewise. Peralta's vaqueros ran them off temporarily, but they returned with a written agreement by which they promised to pay Peralta for the land if he proved that the land was his.

Peralta refused to sign the document and they squatted. Moon and Carpentier were lawyers and the latter eventually gathered a fortune and a very smelly reputation in California before he returned to New York. One historian declared that Carpentier was "free from the slightest trace of honest conviction or the merest scruple of conscience." Major Moon soon fell out with Carpentier, and seems to have eventually become a much respected citizen of Oakland.

Carpentier's approach to solving his problems was through what might be generously termed the governmental process. He can be found with the State Legislature in Vallejo and Sacramento in 1852 in the capacity of Senate Enrollment Clerk. Brief references to his presence indicate that his major accomplishment was in securing the enactment of Chapter 107, an "Act to Incorporate the Town of Oakland and Provide for the Construction of Wharves thereat." The town limits were described by streets represented on Portois' map of Contra Costa, and by bearings from "Oakland House."[14]

Newspapers indicate that some 90 squatters then lived in the vicinity of Oakland House or Hall. That structure was near present Jack London Square, specifically on the northwest corner of Broadway and First (which were then Main and Front streets, respectively). What the residents thought of the new town of Oakland has not been recorded. This law and the town name was probably as much of a surprise to them as it must have been to the legal owners of the land.

Historian Bancroft says that on the strength of a lease which Moon had arranged with Peralta, a townsite was laid out and

---

[14]Jack J. Studer made an intensive study of the conditions of the missing Portois map and the Kellersberger map and plan. His research and historical conclusions are described in two articles in **Cal. Historical Society Quarterly**; March 1968, "Julius Kellersberger: A Swiss Surveyor and City Planner in California, 1851-57;" and also March 1969, "The First Map of Oakland, California: An Historical Speculation as Solution to an Enigma." Studer proposes quite logically that Carpentier had immediate and critical need for a map to accompany his bill to create a Town of Oakland. Clar and his prominent associates had obviously become a formidable hurdle in the path of the squatters. Since the honorable Kellersberger would not allow his unfinished work to be so prostituted, Carpentier used something prepared by a builder named Pierre Portois. The latter's map, if it ever existed in fact, probably was never filed with the Secretary of State.

Andrew Moon hired Kellersberger to make the Oakland plan. Moon's daughter declares (notes deposited with Society of Cal. Pioneers) that Moon built the schoolhouse and wharf and that Carpentier had the record destroyed so that he could claim the waterfront and sell it to the Southern Pacific Company.

Other source material on Oakland development: **Brooklyn Home Journal and Alameda Co. Advertiser** (April 6, 13, 20, 1872); **The Centennial Yearbook of Alameda County**, by Wm. Halley (1876); **Past and Present of Alameda County**, by Joseph E. Baker (1914). Baker implies that Clar and associates were also squatters. They neither squatted nor questioned Peralta's valid ownership. Baker refers to Carpentier (vol. 1, p 355) as a "crafty and unscrupulous lawyer." Leonard Pitt, in his **Decline of the Californios** (1966), pp. 96-98, is more specific and no less critical of Carpentier's behavior.

called Oakland. What happened at the legislature would seem to be quite apart from that transaction, legally speaking. Chapter 107, Statutes of 1852, declared that Oakland was therewith incorporated under a general law of 1850. That basic enabling law provided that any proposed town must have a population of not less than 200. And if the majority were qualified electors who signed a petition which was determined to be proper by the Court of Sessions, the Court could then declare the town incorporated.

Carpentier probably preferred much less publicity than this course required; providing he could have found enough petitioners, which is doubtful. And then there was the slight discomfiture of some legal owners of the proposed town who might have made more of a fuss before the local County Court than would have disturbed the State Legislature of that era.

In Sacramento, where Governor John Bigler signed the act of incorporation into law on May 4, 1852, there was indeed a fascinating little fuss. But no one there seemed to care a whit about the basic honesty of the transaction. The issue involved the matter of granting authority to the proposed five elected town trustees.

Loudest in its castigation of the bill and of Governor Bigler was the San Francisco *Daily Herald*. As the editor saw it, the trustees were given massive dictatorial powers, even unto closing the water approaches to all save favored vessels. And the proposed trustees, as lords of vice, were granted privileges in a law such as no State in this Union had ever dared to enact, said the *Herald*.

The bill, as introduced by Contra Costa County's Napoleon B. Smith, was surely considered and reconsidered for indefinite postponement enough times to be recognized for what it was. Yet it seemed to find friends. In the end, Governor Bigler felt compelled to eventually "yield his approval," as he stated in one of the most remarkable letters of explanation ever penned by a Governor in this State.

Bigler wrote from the Executive Department to the Assembly on May 4, 1852:

> ... This bill contains objectionable features to which I could not have yielded my approval; but there has been laid before me a statement in writing, signed by thirty-two members of the Legislature—representing that the clause in the Act, "Providing for the licensing and restraining of horse racing, gaming houses, and houses of ill-fame", etc. was overlooked in the haste of legislation— and was not intended to license but restrain those houses, and is an error which a subsequent Legislature can easily correct ...

And so it came to pass that regardless of the dubious reputation of some of California's early settlements, none but Oakland can point to the parental blessing of the highest law in the State for the gift of its lusty birthright.[15]

The town council was created. Carpentier was granted several long term privileges provided he build a wharf and school house. These projects were accomplished, but whether by Carpentier or Moon is a moot question.

In the fall of 1852 Carpentier ran for the State Assembly. Some historians estimate there should have been 75 to 150 voters in the area. Carpentier received 519 votes. Two opponents together received a mere 446 votes. One loser challenged the election and the seat was declared vacant. Then a special commission of investigation determined that woodcutters and other unlisted citizens could have accounted for the large vote. Carpentier went to Sacramento as an Assemblyman in 1853. He did not return in 1854.[16]

In the legislative session of 1854 a long, comprehensive, and well composed law was enacted. This continued the business affairs of Oakland town, repealed the original town act and reincorporated the same area as a city. In the new law, an elected mayor and council of six could do many things including "regulate and suppress all occupations, houses, places, amusements and exhibitions which are against good morals. . . . "

Historian Bancroft commented in regard to the new city, "Carpentier managed to get himself elected first mayor. The reported votes numbered 368 which seems excessive for the place at the time, as the census of 1860 allows only 1543 inhabitants."

---

[15]Governor Bigler's letter was printed in the **Journal of the Assembly** for 1852, page 798. The Town of Oakland was not created in the manner provided by the Act of 1850 as stated in the creative act. The enabling act of 1850 made no mention of legislative action. A comparison of Carpentier's handwriting in other State archival documents with the draft of the 1852 Oakland town law presents strong evidence that he was the actual penman who wrote the original bill. There was nothing improper in this; it simply strengthens the opinion stated by others that this was a subject of prime importance to Senate Clerk Carpentier.

[16]State Archives contain the depositions and opinions gathered by the legislative committee of investigation. The committee concluded that since Carpentier received so many votes for the 1853 Assembly office, there surely must be a true majority who favored him. One ferry commuter to San Francisco on election day came forth and told the committee how narrowly he had escaped personal injury when about 30 sturdy gentlemen passengers, through mistaken identity, demanded of him that he pay them the five dollars promised for the several votes each had cast in Oakland township that day.

Bancroft wrote of another Oakland incident which further illustrates the spirit of "squatterism" as he termed it. He says, "The town of Oakland was thrown into a state of great excitement on the 27th of August 1853 arising from the claims of Carpentier, Moore [Moon?] and others to the long line of water property along the front." It seems that 250 citizens met and signed pledges to "divide such property equitably among the people. This, with the assistance of club and pistol they proceeded to do." A big free-for-all fight developed and, wrote Bancroft, ". . . Carpentier's men were beaten and ignominiously driven from the field."

It is interesting that just a month before this incident occurred, San Francisco's *Alta California* published a bitterly sarcastic editorial about the hordes of squatters infesting the Peralta land. In part it stated that "all the lands that were not taken by the squatters last season have been located upon this spring and summer. . . . "

The editor declared that these Americans, " . . . the great, magnanimous, powerful, just people want the lands of the poor and weak, and they take them. . . . It looks hard but we suppose it is fair that these oppressed and outraged citizens should be forcibly dispossessed of their lands, their herds, their orchards and gardens, and at the same time be most onerously taxed for the property thus wrenched from them by force."

The further careers of Carpentier, Moon, and Adams are not of particular interest here. They did pay to Peralta certain sums of money for some property when the Land Claims Commission confirmed the San Antonio Grant in February 1854. It should also be noted that their interests in Peralta holdings extended beyond the limits of that area called Encinal de Temescal. There were also other parties similarly involved. However, a confused situation need not be complicated further to establish the advent of John Clar upon the Contra Costa stage in the fall of 1851.

Peralta declined to sell the Encinal to William Heath Davis whom he must have liked personally. Although he apparently resisted the squatters as well as he could, Peralta's position was rather hopeless in that respect. The eventual selling price seems to have been a secondary matter. Davis and the apologists for the Carpentier faction both complained that their respective offers were in excess of the actual purchase price.

As a passing comment, it might be said that the immediate Spanish ancestry of both Clar and Peralta augured for a *sympatico* relationship. They were the same age. And they had also probably known each other for nearly ten years. Possibly, too, Don Vicente had developed a profound distrust of *Anglos*, not only because of the new squatters, but through his Bear Flag experience. At the time of that uprising at Sonoma in 1846 he, along with General Vallejo, had been taken to Sutter's Fort as a prisoner for a brief time.

Yet, logic points to the case of the general squatter pressure as the most potent argument in favor of Peralta's entering an agreement to sell the Encinal in the fall of 1851. Two months later the purchaser, Clar, was in fact an important technical adviser to the Federal Land Claims Commission. And in that body rested the necessary preliminary assurance of land possession and title.

In the first Book of Deeds at the Recorder's Office in Martinez (there being no County of Alameda at that date) are to be found the miserably handwritten records of the Encinal Land trans-actions. Those wherein Don Vicente was involved are recorded in Spanish. The difficulty of translation rests more in the penman-ship than in the language used.

The translation set forth here was taken from the record of the Supreme Court case mentioned below. It was done for the court by "J. Alexander Forbes, State Translator." The term for money in the original Spanish was pesos and not dollars. For many years in California the terms, and probably the coins, were used interchangeably. The word "Ensinar" was used rather than Encinal in this translation, although court records and historical documents tend to favor the latter word.

> Agreement of bargain and sale that is entered into by and be-tween Mr. Vicente Peralta and Mr. John Clar, on the following con-ditions, witnesseth: 1. Mr. Vicente Peralta sells to Mr. John Clar the portion of my rancho called "Ensinar" which is comprised from the point of the first lake (Laguna) which is near the house of Val-dez in a direct line to the edge of and first point of the canal where the Germans actually are; that is, all the land from this line to the south and up to where are planted this day, two stakes.

> 2d. The price of said Ensinar is ten thousand dollars free from all expenses to said Peralta, and payable three thousand dol-lars cash down, (al contrado) the same which I have received and the remainder until the 13th of January of the coming year, 1852; said land being left under mortage as security for the re-maining seven thousand dollars.

> 3d. Mr. Clar binds himself to prosecute in accordance with the laws of the United States, the squatters that there are upon

the rancho of Peralta, with the object of ejecting them and making them leave the possessions which they have on said rancho, and if the squatters should return after being ejected, Mr. Clar binds himself to execute the proceeding which shall be the decision (of judgment) that may be obtained from the tribunals with respect to said squatters.

4th. Mr. Clar binds himself to leases that Mr. Vicente Peralta has executed with Messrs. Harper & Cook.

5th. Mr. Clar binds himself to comply with all the conditions expressed, without considering as to whether the titles of Peralta are declared good or bad by the commission which the government of the United States may appoint, and to do on his part all that is possible for the validity of said titles.

6th. Mr. Vicente Peralta may take the wood (for fuel) that he may require for his particular use from that portion of the land which is not sold, free from all costs.

Contra Costa, California, 3d Oct., 1851.

VICENTE PERALTA.
JOHN CLAR.

Witnesses present:
MARINO URITO .
EVARISTA E. GAVIN.

Item 4 of the contract obviously applied to some form of lease upon the Encinal entered into earlier by Peralta and Harper and Cook.

It should also be noted in item 3 that *el rancho de Peralta* was the term used, and not just the Encinal. In this respect the purchaser and his later associates failed to meet the terms of the agreement. Under the prevailing circumstances the only practical remedy of meeting the squatter invasion was to encourage the prompt confirmation of the original San Antonio Grant by the Land Claims Commission. The fact that Deputy Surveyor-General Alexy von Schmidt was instructed to survey the rancho boundary in the spring of 1852 can be viewed as a token of good faith (as well as being highly desirable to those interested and influential parties, Clar and Jack Hays).

Unfortunately, no memoranda regarding personal discussions between Peralta and Clar during 1850 and 1851 are known to exist. There is, however, the record of a particular case at law which reveals one aspect of the preliminaries of this land transaction. This was the case of Mrs. Harriet Truett versus Edson Adams, which was in the courts from 1877 through 1884. The fact that some

Contrata de Compra y Venta que celebran los Sn Dn
Vicente Peralta y Mr John Clar bajo las condiciones siguien-
tes

1º  Dn Vicente Peralta vende a Mr John Clar la parte de
mi rancho llamada Encinar comprendida desde la
punta de la primera laguna que esta cerca de la casa
de Balsas linea recta a la orilla y punta primera del
canal donde estan los alemanes actualmente esto es todo
el terreno de de esta linea al sur y donde quedan planta-
dos hoi mismos dos estacas

2º  El precio de dicho Encinar es diez mil pesos libres de
todo gasto pª Peralta y pagaderos tres mil al Contado
los mismos que hoi he recibido y el resto dia trece
de Enero del año entrante 1852 quedando hipotecado
dicho terreno en garantia de los siete mil pesos restantes.

3º  Mr Clar se obliga a perseguir segun las leys de
los Estados Unidos a los squaters que hoi en el rancho
de Peralta con el objeto de espulsarlos y hacerles dejar
las posesiones que tienen en dicho rancho y si los squaters volvieren despues de haberlos espulsado Mr Clar
se obliga a ejecutar los procedimientos que sera la
sentencia que se obtenga de los tribunales respeto de dichos
squaters

4º  Mr Clar se obliga a respetar los contratos de arriendo
que Dn Vicente Peralta tiene celebrado con Mr
Harper y Cook.

5º  Mr Clar se obliga a cumplir con todos las condiciones espresadas sin atender a si los titulos de Peralta
seran declarados buenos o malos por la Comision que
nombre el gobierno de los Estados Unidos y a hacer
de mi parte cuanto sea posible para la validez
de dichos titulos

6º  La leña que Dn Vicente Peralta necesita para su
uso particular podra tomarle de la parte del
terreno que no sea vendido sin costo ninguno
Contra costa California Octubre trece de mil ochocientos
cincuenta y uno.

Bicente Peralta
John Clar

Testigos presenciales
Mariano Urita
Evaristo E Garin

Original Peralta-Clar Agreement
— Contra Costa County Records

of the witness testimony was in direct opposition does not detract from its historical value.

Note the quoted land description in the first item of the Encinal contract of sale. When the California Supreme Court gave an opinion in this case it was generous in concluding that the description "was not free from ambiguity." And that is why Mrs. Truett claimed she owned land on the Encinal which, she said, was *not* sold by Peralta within the described area, and which land Edson Adams assumed he had acquired by due process sometime after 1852.

This brings forth a most baffling question in respect to John Clar's many activities. This man probably had no peer in California in his comprehension of the nuances of the Spanish tongue, and in land subdivision terminology. Why did he accept such a vague and general land description? Naturally, there were no existing government monuments to be used as reference points. But the references and the descriptive words used even for that time and place seem most inadequate. Perhaps Don Vicente himself was sensitive as to the wording. The document was, of course, drafted only in the Spanish version.

As a matter of fact, another individual claimed under oath that he had written the Encinal contract. This person was most certainly the occupant of "the house of Valdez." José M. Valdez came to California about 1846. When or under what circumstance he was permitted to reside on Peralta property is not known. Early Contra Costa County land records do not reveal any transfer of property by lease or sale from Peralta to José M. Valdez. He did come to own the valuable land from 20th to 28th streets, Harrison to Broadway, Oakland.

The old house location can be generally fixed near the north end of present Lake Merritt, near Valdez Street and north of Grand Avenue. A quarter century after the event, Valdez appeared as the principal and practically the sole witness on behalf of Mrs. Truett.

He had written the document, declared Valdez, and further, he and two partners named Callijas and Escanila had persuaded Clar, a good friend of Peralta, to act as their agent and purchase the Encinal. The three of them provided the 3000 pesos down payment. Clar provided nothing. In fact, the latter had even failed to chase away the squatters, declared the witness. In the Supreme

Court record it would appear that Valdez offered these particular bits of information gratuitously and outside of counsel's questions.

That record contains only one cross-examination query in response to the Valdez revelation. He was asked what he knew about the actual deed which was executed five and one-half months later. He replied that he knew nothing of it.

Well over a century has passed since this alleged happening. Perhaps other evidence exists that would cause Señor Valdez and friends to be listed as a fourth party of interest in the acquisition of the Encinal de Temescal. The firm court evidence indicates that no other witness sustained his allegations, and further, the District (Superior) Court of Alameda and the State Supreme Court appear to have totally ignored his testimony.

The court judgment was specifically related to the question of whether the area intended to be described was limited on the east and west by lines running due south from the stakes of record. Valdez said, "yes." John Clar and a number of others said they had never understood any such limitations. The courts said, "no."

Valdez said that he and Peralta and Clar and one other (whom he could not recall) rode around the entire Encinal prior to the signing of the contract. Clar said that he had not driven the stakes. They were already there and Peralta pointed them out. When asked why they were put where they were, Clar replied that they were logically placed at the water's edge. On the west side was a tidal marsh or slough intruding inland 1950 feet from the low tide common shore line. On the east, several small lakes and wet depressions extended westward from the later named Lake Merritt about 1400 feet. This was the reason for the stakes. They were line stakes and not corner monuments, although no one seems to have stated the fact very clearly in the testimony of record.

The identity of "the Germans" was not revealed. One witness named Edward Gibbons mentioned a "John Frees and another partner" occupying a house on the bay side.

Among prominent witnesses on behalf of Adams came Horace Carpentier. The record notes that he and John Clar each held in his hands the original contract document and testified as to its validity. Two things Carpentier said from the witness chair are of interest. He said, "Adams and I were squatters," and that there were 40 or 50 people on the Encinal in the 1851-52 period.

## EAST BAY SURVEY OF 1852

Upon the instructions of Surveyor-General King, Deputy Surveyor Alexy W. von Schmidt ran a compass and chain course around the Rancho San Antonio of Don Luis Peralta. This was completed in August of 1852, five months after the sale of Encinal de Temescal to John Clar, **et al.,** and three months after the State Legislature created a Town of Oakland. This survey was unquestionably the first accurate delineation of the San Antonio Rancho boundary.

The map area reproduced here covers only the central portion of the grant. The Encinal de Temescal lies on the north side of the creek or estuary of San Antonio.

Survey stations occupied by von Schmidt are marked along the edge of the Bay, along the summit of the Berkeley Hills, and down Temescal Creek. The outer boundary was the primary concern of the Land Claims Commission. Some internal features on the map were no doubt established by rough triangulation during the exterior survey.

The white space at upper left is simply a missing part of the map. Note the home ranch of Vicente Peralta in the triangle formed by the space and Temescal Creek. At a later date Telegraph Avenue was established along the west side of these buildings. Claremont Avenue came in from the northeast to join Telegraph about four city blocks to the south of the ranch structures.

The ranch headquarters of brother Antonio, with orchard and garden, are clearly marked on San Antonio Creek. Directly east of "Oak Land City," along the hills are the trees generally called Peralta's Red Woods. By 1852 logging operations were removing these giants from their prominent place on the **contra costa** skyline.

The heavy concentration of trees sketched by von Schmidt at the two places called "encinals" or oak groves, and the dearth of such symbols elsewhere is strong evidence of the general open character of this pasture land.

Peralta thought of the Encinal as a peninsula, bounded on the west by the bay, and on the south and east by the estuary. The north boundary was established as a straight line about two miles in length, running North 63 degrees West from the upper, inner estuary to San Francisco Bay. This was called the Encinal Line of 1852. The total area thus enclosed probably embraced 1600 acres above the mud flats and marshes.

The Peralta-Clar deed describes this line as running between these two points: ". . . from the point of the first lake, which is near the house of Valdez, in a direct line to the edge and first point of the canal where the Germans actually are . . ."

The Encinal Line can be reasonably reconstructed on this map by accepting the house at the isolated clump of trees at the map center as the Valdez house. This was presumably located around present Valdez Street and Grand Avenue, Oakland. Little is known of "the Germans" over on the bay side. Von Schmidt indicated what might be the mouth of a canal or slough precisely where he began lettering the words "salt marsh." Generally the line extended from the north end of present Lake Merritt to near the Bay Bridge Toll Plaza.

Red Woods

Antonio Peralta

San Antonio Creek

A general reconstruction of the Encinal Line of 1852 would place it as beginning on the shore of Lake Merritt north of present Kaiser Center, and extending westward about 63 degrees west of north to a point between the present Bay Bridge Toll Plaza and the highway traffic distribution structure to the east. One may presume that one of the stakes of record was driven about where Peralta Street intersects Nimitz Freeway. Topographic maps as late as 1915 indicate swampy land there. The other stake on the east could have been set at about present Grand Avenue and Broadway. The area south of the Encinal Line to the Estuary constituted the block of land termed the Encinal, although there were other "oak groves," even as near as Alameda. The adjoining area north of the Encinal Line was generally termed the Temescal. This line also separated the so-called peninsula from the mainland.[17]

It would be interesting to know if the official Surveyor of Marin County was able to produce his own 3000 pesos (or dollars) for the original down payment. (If Señor Valdez did in fact make that payment he should later have charged Clar with fraud, deception and grand theft.) The contract called for payment of the remaining 7000 pesos to Peralta by January 13, 1852. Unquestionably, John Clar needed financial assistance.

Biographer Greer says that Clar approached Colonel Hays because of his money problem. It is also very probable that the tough political strength and recognized moral integrity of Sheriff

---

[17]Records of the Truett v. Adams case may be seen in Alameda Co. Court House (Case No. 5083); in State Archives Supreme Court file 16476; in Supreme Court 66 Cal 218. The latter contains detailed reference to land area terminology.

The final ruling in this case was vitally important in clearing numerous cloudy land titles. Because no trial transcript was found, comments of historical value are mostly from appeal documents prepared by plaintiff's attorney. One of his major objectives must have been to identify Clar as a mere agent in the Encinal purchase, and therefore not a highly competent witness. On the other hand, the attorney seemed to avoid having Clar's personal integrity or knowledge of the Spanish language become a point at issue, even in deepest sarcasm. For example (Case 5083, page 7): "Plaintiff cannot afford to have her rights sworn away by such **disinterested** and accomplished scholars as Hall and Clar, who treat dictionaries and grammars as though they were blank paper. There cannot be found a Spaniard in California who will not contradict Hall."

One unusual document in the same file is the Truett attorney's statement or memo addressed to the judge which sets forth what one of the Galindo kin **would** have said as the prime witness to the Peralta-Clar negotiation on the ground, had not the early adjournment of court interfered. A casual comparison of this averred Galindo statement with the trial testimony of Valdez raises some question as to their consistency. If this Galindo had been the man Valdez failed to remember on the horseback ride around the Encinal, surely the attorney would have caused him to recollect and so testify.

Jack Hays were no less valuable in this particular struggle. At any rate, from this time on, Hays played an important part in the Oakland story.[18]

Sheriff Hays had been living about thirty miles south of San Francisco, to which city he commuted daily on horseback. When he crossed the Bay and rode over the hills to see the Oakland area he decided that this was where he wished to live. And he did so, until his death in 1883.

The actual sale transaction from Peralta to Clar and associates occurred on March 13, 1852. This was two months before Governor Bigler's signature in Sacramento created a Town of Oakland. Before considering the details it would be well to note three recorded sales of property made by Clar *before* March of that year 1852.

One transaction in particular is especially difficult to comprehend. On February 7, 1852, Clar conveyed "all of my right, title interest and claim. . . to that certain tract. . . known by the name of Encinal. . . unto Joseph K. Irving. . . for the Sum of Ten Thousand Dollars. . . . "

It is possible that this was actually a mortgage, but it has the appearance of a quitclaim deed. One historian states that it was the latter. Yet, the primary deed would tend to prove otherwise. And incidentally, Thomas A. Brown, Recorder, wished to have the record show that he had "affixed my private seal there being no seal provided for the office."

It should also be noted that a certain Blakely Kelly, a "competent and credible witness" identified two witnesses to the signing. Probably Blakely Kelly was known to Brown because in another document dated November 28, 1851, John Clar had deeded to the aforesaid Kelly ". . . a house and lot in the Town of Contra Costa now unlawfully occupied by Edward [Andrew?] Moon, the lot not to exceed 100 feet square. . . . "

On January 22, 1852, John Clar did, for the consideration of one hundred dollars, grant, bargain and sell to one William N. Brown, both parties being residents of San Francisco, that certain parcel of land "at a place now called Contra Costa on a creek

[18]Some Hays business papers are deposited at Cal. Hist. Society Library. Among several hundred old checks are a half-dozen clearly related to Oakland. These are on forms of Bankinghouse of Palmer, Cook and Company; signed by John Freaner and Thomas Johnson, undoubtedly representing Hays. One check dated April 3, 1854, provides payment to "Interest on Clar's 3 notes. Seventy-five dollars, acct Oakland Purchase."

or slough called San Antonio. . .and near a house now called Oakland Hall and upon which land now hereby conveyed a wharf is now constructed or partially so. . . ."

The description very clearly embraced a lot 80 feet wide and 160 feet long of which the wharf was the central part and the principal witness monument.

Thus did Mr. Moon's house and Mr. Carpentier's wharf change ownership by these somewhat anticipatory sales initiated by the presumptive land owner of record, John Clar. It would be interesting to know the actual effect of these duly recorded sales in that period of entrenched squatterism. One thing again appears evident: the legal owners must have been surprised when the squatter community they knew as Contra Costa was abruptly christened Oakland by State statute a few months later.

As stated, the actual sale of Encinal was completed on March 13, 1852. The document was written in Spanish and signed by three persons; Vicente Peralta, John Clar, and with her mark, Encarnación G. de Peralta. Harper, who was mentioned in the original contract, was a Justice of the Peace. He recorded (in English) the appearance before him of the three principals to the transaction. He stated that Señora Peralta, "being of full age," was questioned apart from Don Vicente to assure that she was acting "without any coercion or compulsion of her husband."

The so-called community property law was of Spanish origin, and it was being respected by the new American State in this case. It seems, however, that husbands assumed superior rights in the management of community property.

The recorded deed read as follows:

> Let it be known by this instrument of sale that I, Vicente Peralta, in consideration of the sum of ten thousand ($10,000) dollars, which have been paid to me cash in hand, and to my satisfaction in accordance with the annexed contract with John Clar, have bargained, sold and transferred to the named Clar one portion of the land called "Ensinar" which is described in said contract. The said Clar having declared that he has one-fourth part, of which one-third belongs to B. de la Barra, one-fourth part to J. K. Irving, another one-fourth part to Messrs. John C. Hays and John Caperton, and another one-fourth part to Jacob Alexander Cost.

Already in accordance with the declaration of Mr. John Clar, and for the consideration before named, by these presents, I sell, transfer, and convey and grant to the aforesaid parties that portion of land already mentioned, to wit:

John Clar . . . . . . . 1/6 part.
To B. de la Barra, . . . . 1/12 ”
J. K. Irving . . . . . . 1/4 ”
Messrs. John C. Hays . .
   and John Caperton, . 1/4 ”
Jacob Alexander Cost, . . 1/4 ”

In order that they and their heirs may possess the said land without there being any claim by me, or my heirs, concerning the aforesaid sale.

Contra Costa Co., March 13th, 1852.

VICENTE PERALTA,
ENCARNACION G. DE PERALTA,
JOHN CLAR,

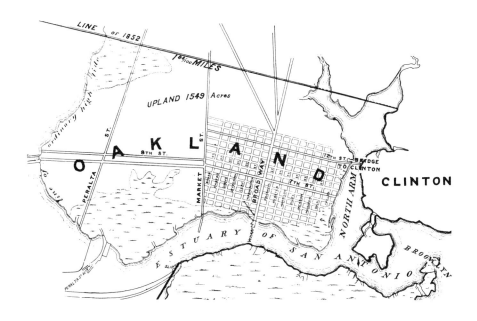

Oakland About 1872
— California State Archives

The Oakland Town incorporation act of May 4, 1852, drew at least one clear public challenge. On the front page of the San Francisco *Daily Herald* of May 19 appeared the following advertisement:

> BARRETT & SHERWOOD,
> ap25tf City Observatory, Clay st.
>
> CAUTION to the Public.—The undersigned being the sole owners of the Encinal in Contra Costa county, opposite San Francisco, by purchase from Vicente Peralta, hereby warn the public against purchasing from any other parties pretending to claim said land,
> JOHN C. HAYS,
> JOHN CAPERTON,
> J. A. COST,
> J. R. IRVING,
> my13tf J. CLAR.
>
> OPPOSITE San Francisco — For Sale, a por-

The same newspaper page offered land for sale by Chipman and Aughinbaugh on the Encinal San Antonio, more commonly known as the Bolsa or Peninsula del Encinal, and later as Alameda. For some reason squatters did not overwhelm these purchasers who had paid Antonio Peralta "good lawful American money" for the land south of the estuary.

Incidentally, during 1852 a passenger steamer named *Red Jacket* was making three round trips daily between San Francisco and Embarcadero San Antonio at "Oakland City."

Just what John Clar made or lost in the Oakland venture is not known. It appears that he was holding a one-sixth interest when in August of 1853 the associates partitioned that portion of the City of Oakland which they claimed. Thereafter the story becomes lost in litigation and time.

In obituary notices, two San Francisco newspapers used these same words, "In early days he became possessor of the site of the town of Oakland. The property was, however, wrested from him piece by piece, by overreaching speculations." This writer's father always heatedly denied such an allegation, which would seem to indicate that some profit was realized. Presumably there was just a little more truth in the *Examiner's* words at this time, "In those early days Captain Clar bought a great deal of land, which he afterward sold at what was considered a good profit." There is no record, however, that he made any other than the Encinal purchase. But then, there is the story of Clarville yet to be told.

# 8   A Man of All Work

$\mathcal{B}$etween the Oakland problems and the increasing work load at the Office of Surveyor-General, John Clar must have been a busy man during the early 1850's. He assumed a further serious obligation in his fortieth year.

It is now our pleasure to introduce a lovely Parisian girl named Angèle Lesgent. She was 21 years of age in 1853.

Many Europeans were leaving their troubled homelands in the 1850's and migrating to America. Some of them developed a substantial French community in San Francisco where a number of the earlier pioneers of old Yerba Buena had been Frenchmen. It is known that Mademoiselle Lesgent came from a middle class family of silver manufacturers and jewelers and it is said that she was in the company of an uncle and aunt on a world tour. Among such vaporous family recollections there yet persists the legend of her youthful beauty and angelic disposition. Two plaintive notes of farewell from her homeland have been preserved. On July 27, 1852, in Paris, the soul of one Ernest L'Abbé is revealed in this fading script: *"Je vous aime.* I have hoped very much. And tomorrow you are going away, leaving us for a long time, perhaps. . . ."

Nothing has been recorded of the romance between the 40-year-old government employee and the *Parisienne*, except that they were married on October 20, 1853, in the home of French Consul Patrice Dillon, by the Right Reverend Archbishop Alemany. After his four years residence in San Francisco it is of interest that John Clar is recorded in local newspapers as being of Norfolk, Virginia. The term Californian still referred to the old provincial Mexican residents.[19]

---

[19]Notes are in possession of granddaughter Elizabeth Zuchelli of Modesto. A beautiful wedding present given to the Clars from persons unknown may be viewed at the Society of Cal. Pioneers' exhibit room. This is a Bohemian glass tray and decanter set, donated by great-granddaughter Angele Beatrice Shaw Colthorpe of Tucson.

A few hours before the Clar wedding there was a marriage celebrated across the bay in which William Pinkney Toler joined Maria Antonia Peralta, niece of Vicente. Midshipman Toler had been Professor Clar's scholar aboard the **Cyane** and **Savannah** and had enjoyed the unusual distinction of having personally raised the American flag with Jones in 1842 and again with Sloat in 1846.

Angele (Lesgent) Clar
circa 1865

Undoubtedly, the prominent Archbishop Joseph S. Alemany had had much business association with the bridegroom during the recent year. That reverend gentleman was making numerous small representations on behalf of the Christianized Indians of California before the Land Claims Commission. More precisely the land he represented involved the remnants of the original mission holdings. He was also assigned the difficult task of practically reconstructing a system of parish churches after the devastating secularization program of the 1830's. But that is a different and very complex story of this era.

San Francisco's first Catholic Archbishop and John Clar were both born in Spain at almost the same time. At any rate, it is difficult to ascribe any motive other than personal friendship for this courtesy of the high prelate in performing the marriage ceremony. There is ample testimony of the bridegroom's personal charm, but in material wealth, political prestige and religious orthodoxy he was churchmouse poor.

Early directories of San Francisco indicate that the newlyweds lived on Sutter Street near Powell and Stockton. The Land Office was located at Kearney and Washington streets.

During the course of some seventeen years a number of sons were born to this couple. Several died in infancy. Seven records of birth have been discovered. Four sons grew to maturity and advanced age.

A government employee in any department had practically no assurance of tenure in office during this period. The Department of Interior seemed to suffer especially from this spoils system of firing and hiring relatives and political friends.

In the 1850's a secret political faction of anti-foreign, anti-Catholic, ultra-Americans developed in the Eastern States. The principal victims of this so-called Know Nothing Party were the Irish immigrants who, in their dire poverty, were depressing the value of both free and slave labor.

In California by 1854 this true-blue agglomerate of Americans was officially known as the American Political Party. The party composition was somewhat different in the new West. Ironically, many Irish names were prominent here where "foreigners" were unwelcome competitors in the "Golden Triangle." This region was bounded by the Northern and Southern Mines of the Mother Lode with San Francisco at the apex. Circumstances made it inevitable that most vulnerable to abuse and property loss during the sometimes violent behavior of the Know Nothings were the native-born *Californios*. It is doubtful if many new arrivals among the *Anglos* made an effort to distinguish between Sonorans, Chileans, California Spanish, or even French immigrants. The *Californios* on their part possibly gained a little personal satisfaction by designating the Know Nothings as the *Ignorantes*.

In the elections of 1854 the American Party swept State offices including the governorship. Its candidates also captured most of the local offices in the north. It is quite probable, however, that the majority of voters had more hope of improving the miserable standards of political morality in government than interest in the anti-foreign principles of the party.

The hope for improvement failed to materialize and the Know Nothings as a political party quickly degenerated. Its strong echoes were soon to reappear, however, with the Chinese coolie as the new target of abuse.

Because of the agitation stirred up by the campaign oratory and the actual confrontations between "Yankees" and "foreigners," a government employee of obvious Spanish ancestry could have met with embarrassment. At any rate, on the 22nd day of October,

1855, one John Clar, a native of Spain did, in the U. S. District Court of San Francisco, acquire citizenship by formal procedure. It appears quite certain that no one had deemed this to be necessary during his years of service as a naval officer and government employee. It is also to be noted that one of the primary conditions set forth in both Federal and California law for any person who wished to settle upon the public lands and claim a homestead was American citizenship.

Among the few written records left by John Clar, other than official goverment documents, was the notebook he kept at the Land Office.[20] Unfortunately, the book contains little of profound historical importance. Its time period is well fixed by the beautiful scribing of the author's name, the place, and the date "July 1st 1853" on the leading page, and a pale pencil notation on the last page that "L. Upson left Cal Feb 26, 1866."

The book was obviously used to jot down working notes about places and things common to land papers, and reference to those laws and regulations pertaining to land surveying and measurement, both Mexican and American.

The annotator was much more concerned about the true length of the California *vara* than the old *rancheros* had ever been. Legend has it that any land measurement undertaken was probably accomplished with a rawhide *reata* dragging behind a saddlehorse. Undoubtedly this story originated in the rough but reasonable measuring system conducted by two horsemen. Each carried a pole, between which a rawhide cord was suspended. This "cordele" was generally 50 *varas*, or approximately 150 feet in length. Progress along an accepted course was made in leap-frog fashion, moving the rear pole forward two *cordeles* and sticking it into the ground where it would soon become the rear pole again. At any rate, whether the *vara* was 33 English inches as the Land Office first prescribed, or 33.372 as John Clar calculated as being more proper, could have been of little concern in the pleasant land before the restive *Anglos* came.

How did a *ranchero* determine the length of his measuring stick or rawhide rope? Supposedly he could check the length of a true *vara* from the marks on the staff of office of the nearest alcalde.

---

[20]The book is deposited at Bancroft Library.

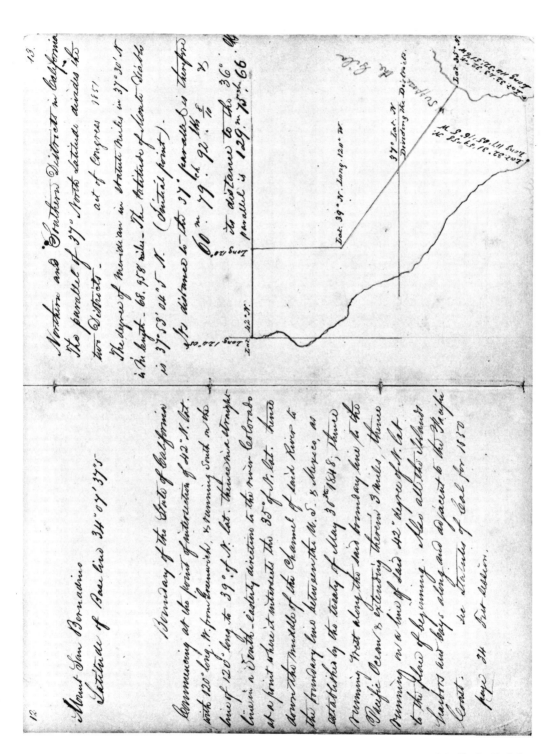

John Clar's Notebook

There are also a number of personal things noted in the book, such as a problem of navigation; some translations into several languages; remedies for toothache, neuralgia, rheumatism; and dubious hair dressing composed of sugar of lead (enough to cover a bit coin), sulfur and bay rum. The man was beginning to suffer intensely from the pains of arthritis at this time.

To the general public the name most familiar among contemporary government surveyors must have been that of Alexey von Schmidt, later honored by the military rank of colonel. At the present day a few knowing persons will immediately associate him with the so-called "Von Schmidt Line" which was the first boundary survey between Nevada and California running from Lake Tahoe to the Colorado River. But in the spring of 1870 he was the toast of San Francisco following his success in blowing the top off the treacherous Blossom Rock which was below the water surface about a mile off Telegraph Hill. This underwater demolition was hailed as a remarkable engineering feat of that day. It has been said that John Clar assisted in the project.

The San Francisco *Examiner*, in the review of Clar's life at the time of his death declared, "When the boundary line between Califorina and Nevada was about to be established, Colonel von Schmidt asked Captain Clar to participate in the work, but the latter's health was so poor that he could not endure the work and exposure." That survey was made in 1872.[21]

No doubt the two surveyors were longtime congenial friends, each respecting the other's ability. But at some time, probably soon after 1853, Captain Clar became irritated with contract surveyor von Schmidt. He wrote down the cause. Then later he considered it judicious to blot out the name of the erring surveyor. However, for sake of historical accuracy it can be reported by the third generation snoopers that the name von Schmidt is unquestionably to be read under the pen scratches in the old notebook.

The irritation was justified. The deputy surveyor had forgotten to make adjustments along the standard parallels to provide for the convergence of true north-south lines due to earth curvature. Considerable adjoining work of land-sectionizing was in danger of facing rejection. One can still feel the schoolmaster's

[21]This was a difficult project, technically and physically. See "The Oblique Boundary Line Between California and Nevada" by C. H. Sinclair in U.S.C. & G.S. Survey Report of 1900.

wrath in this closing sentence of the notation, "Deputies should understand the properties of the Sphere and other subjects connected with surveying — They would thus avoid errors so serious and grave, and which cannot be made to disappear from the public records."

The Society of California Pioneers archival records contain this copy of a letter which is difficult to read because of the handwriting. Its meaning is nevertheless quite clear. The letter was addressed to "Hon. Thomas A. Hendricks, Com. Gen. Land Office, Washington, D. C."

———

U. S. Sur Gen Office
San Francisco, Cal
April 4, 1856

Sir:

I have the honor to acknowledge the receipt of your communication of the 18 February last, in which you make certain inquiries and suggestions as to the propriety of the further continuance of a translator in this office. The gentleman heretofore denominated "keeper of the old archives and translator" Mr. John Clar, has been like some of my other clerks "a man of all work". Spanish is his vernacular tongue, yet he has been in the employ of our Government for more than twenty years as a linguist and mathematician.

I think it can safely be asserted that there is not on the Pacific coast, a more correct translator of the Spanish into English, nor a more ready and practical mathematician than he is.

His services in this office have become, and are more indispensable when I say his place cannot be spared.

More than ever I shall need a man of his superior qualifications in detail of the examinations of the original documents and title papers referred to in the confirmation of the commissioners transfers—along [with] making instructions for the survey of Mexican claims, and also in the examination of their intricate calculations appertaining to the surveys when restored.

Instead of a decrease in the business consequent upon the dissolution of the Land Commission and the turning over of their papers and documents to this office, the increase in so far immense, and the duties of those entrusted with them necessarily onerous.

In the view of the necessity existing for the continued services of Mr. Clar I sincerely hope and trust the Department will deem it expedient, and for the best interests of the Government to per-

mit to continue him in his present situation and at the salary heretofore allowed him, as I must say that any change would deprive
the office of his services I should consider a most serious public evil.

> Very respectfully
> Your obt. Servnt.
> John C. Hays
> U.S. Surv. Gen. Cal.

The Land Claims Commission had been officially liquidated
on March 3, 1855, with the U. S. Surveyor-General in San Francisco
designated as its successor. The preliminary hearings regarding
validity of rancho claims had been accomplished, but many bitter
issues remained unsolved. The justification of Hay's appeal is
supported by the historical fact that for more than thirty years
following this letter of 1856 there was in the Land Office at San
Francisco a position Keeper of Archives and Translator.

In fact, on August 29, 1883, John Clar, above his title of
Keeper of Spanish Archives and Translator, compiled a "succinct
account" of the status of Spanish archives at that date in the California Office of U. S. Surveyor General. He listed several major
designations of catalogued land records and then referred to "some
300 ponderous volumes, mostly in manuscript" pertaining to the
Spanish era. He informed Surveyor-General W. H. Brown that this
material "contains valuable information for the historian and man
of letters, yet no Digest of their contents has ever been made. . . .
It would take fully two years to accomplish."[22]

Regardless of the value of his work in the mind of Surveyor-
General Hays in 1856, Clar suffered a severe salary reduction about
the first of October. He seems to have worked as a draftsman for
half of the following year, prior to his "discharge" on October 5,
1857. Hays had retired on September 8th.

Ostensibly, the departure of Hays indicated the conclusion
of a four-year political appointment. More than likely the political
pot had boiled over. James Buchanan had taken office as President in March of 1857. Possibly because of the local popularity of

---

[22]The original letter was possessed by Mrs. Keith Ponsford of Oakland when she
furnished a copy to this writer in 1969. She is the granddaughter of Valentin Alviso,
the last keeper of Old Archives. Had Alviso not removed the letter from official files
it would have been lost along with the described land records in the fire of 1906.
It seems logical that this particular letter was written for the same reason that
inspired the A.M. Kenady letter only 18 days later, namely, to illustrate the worth
of this government employee. However, its administrative value to Alviso a few
years after that is quite obvious.

Hays or his reputation as a law enforcement man, or both, Buchanan offered him a similar position in the Utah Territory. This region was then in a near state of armed rebellion against the United States.

Although the amazing Colonel Hays had permitted an expenditure considerably in excess of the sum appropriated for land subdivision work he seemed to have suffered little condemnation from any direction in California. His reputation for rugged honesty and the great need to get on with the fixing of firm land titles caused all interested parties to request the new federal administration to leave him in the California office. Yet, Buchanan promptly appointed James W. Mandeville Surveyor-General of California.

Hays resigned the Utah appointment without ever having made a move to accept it. He did, however, recognize that appointment as virtually an official acknowledgment of his own personal integrity. And he did travel to Washington to explain why it was urgently necessary to take the final step in the confirmation of grant lands. Establishing ownership was one thing. Designating true land boundaries was also a problem in many cases.

Hays should have found more personal business to attend in his East Bay land development than even his huge energy could meet. Yet he apparently agreed to act as a deputy to the Surveyor-General for the purpose of surveying the external boundaries of a dozen or more of the confirmed ranchos. One of them was the Tzábaco Rancho which was adjacent to, or which embraced the present village of Geyserville in Sonoma County. And the determination of that very point of location will constitute the essential subject of the following chapter.

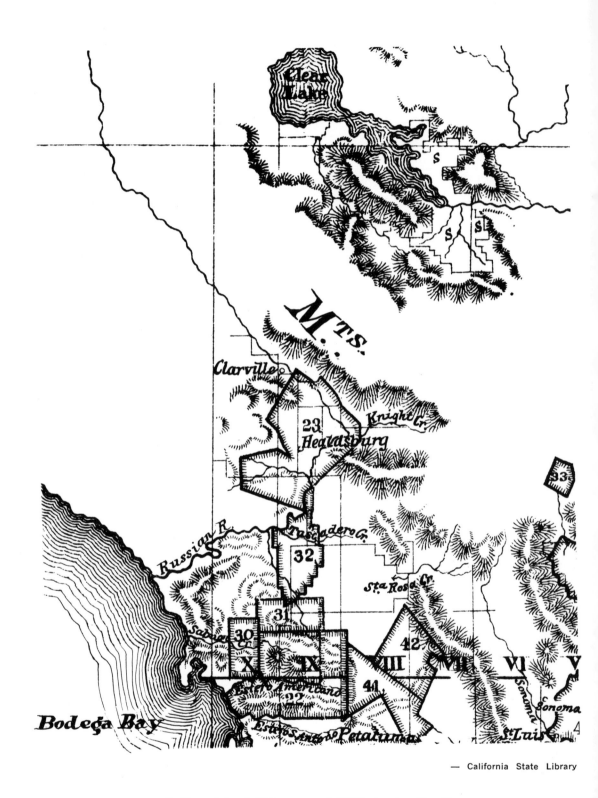

— California State Library

Portion of Land Office map of 1857 showing Clarville
at the center. See page 123.

# 9   Clarville

hree conditions affected the settler or squatter situation along the Russian River around present Geyserville which were different from the San Antonio Rancho case on the east shore of San Francisco Bay. The Peralta lands were extremely desirable and vulnerable to a great number of land seekers. The intensity of the deluge there occurred at an earlier time, a matter of some five very eventful years, and before the State legislature was so influenced by squatter power. The actual land boundaries of the San Antonio were never a point of contention; while external bounds of Tzábaco Rancho were the primary question. That particular question presents an excellent example of the great burden assumed by the Land Claims Commission in trying to comprehend and adjudicate where vague property descriptions were presumed to have been drawn at a time when land had little monetary value and people upon the land were few in number.

An attempt will be made in this chapter to relate how the Peña family first requested and then acquired the property still identified by the name Tzábaco in Sonoma County. It is a very complicated story and it is best to start with an explanation of the general legal conditions under which settlers went upon and acquired the public lands of this State and the United States.

Settlement upon the virgin land was a basic element in the development of the United States as a gestating nation. Homesteading laws provided legitimacy for the taking of roots upon the new continent by most of the restless families which had from colonial days begun to push into the wilderness toward the setting sun.

The Congress enacted in 1841 a Pre-emption Act, and in 1862 the more familiar Homestead Act. There were other somewhat similar federal laws. A primary facet of the pre-emption law was its provision that the settler, or squatter if you please, would enter a formal claim when the land was sectionized by government survey. The claimant must be a citizen; the claim could not exceed 160 acres; and the price to be paid to the government was fixed at $1.25 per acre.

The point of interest in respect to the California situation of the 1850's is that the young State government felt compelled to create similar and independent laws. This was a time and place of great change and controversy. An entire new system of government had to be created by the wide spectrum of new citizens, and a few of the old. A great civil war was on the horizon, and its tearing passions had been transferred into the new land in the hearts of its immigrants. Midst the numerous and exciting problems of self-government the problem of settlement upon the land was definitely not the least.

At the first session of the California Legislature in 1849-50, there was enacted a Chapter 83 which was titled "An Act prescribing the mode of maintaining and defending Possessory Actions on lands belonging to the United States." This law provided that any person might occupy and settle upon unoccupied public land provided it did not contain mines or precious metal. The claimant could not occupy more than 160 acres and he must mark boundaries on the ground. If he neglected to occupy or cultivate his claim for a period of three months the land would be considered abandoned.

This law was enlarged considerably in 1852 through Chapter 82. Now the reason of settlement was to be for the purpose of cultivating or grazing the land. The new State law repeated the essential federal requirements of pre-emption homesteading. A claimant was required to file with the County Recorder and give a reasonable description of his settlement. This provided a more secure official recording. It also placed the property on the official tax assessment roll.

It was also provided that a settler could leave his claim for a period not exceeding one year. However, if he were absent for more than 60 days without having made a payment of 15 dollars to the County Treasurer his claim would be considered abandoned.[23]

---

[23]In that same legislative session of 1852 the lengthy Chapter 4 was enacted into law. This provided that the State could sell $500,000 in warrants to prospective settlers upon government land which was, or which would be granted to the State of California. The warrants sold at the rate of two dollars for each acre intended to be settled upon, but not exceeding 320 acres for any one person. All income was transferred into a special school fund.

A temporary description of boundaries would serve until the government surveyors fixed the final location of the claimed property. Land found to be in Spanish or Mexican grants was not to be "prejudiced" by this law. However, it was provided that should the settler's claim be determined to be not on open land of the United States, then the warrant holder could "float" his claim to "any other public lands in the State of California."

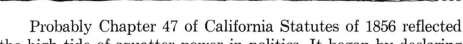 

Probably Chapter 47 of California Statutes of 1856 reflected the high tide of squatter power in politics. It began by declaring that "All lands of this State shall be deemed and regarded as public lands until the legal title is shown to have passed from the Government to private citizens."

It was further provided that the rights of a patentee "shall be deemed to begin at the patent and he shall not be entitled to recover for the use or enjoyment of such land prior to the date of such patent." As though this were not a sufficient invitation to plunder rancho lands not yet fully confirmed, other sections of law provided that the defendant squatter could take action to resist ejectment. In the event he lost his case he could make a claim for recovery of the value of his own improvements made upon the land, and he was entitled to reimbursement, as fixed by the court within a period of six months thereafter.

The owners of confirmed and patented Spanish and Mexican grant lands, and patentees of land acquired from the State, were not to be jeopardized by squatters, *provided* their land had been surveyed, plainly marked along boundaries, and all the survey and patent records formally recorded in the particular county. Further, those persons who used force to occupy grant land enclosed by a fence could not expect aid and comfort under this Settler's Protection Act of 1856.

Then in 1858, after the State Supreme Court had chopped away some of the power of squatters, Chapter 358 was enacted as balm for some wounds. This law provided "for the better protection of settlers on Public Lands in this State and to secure the rights of parties in certain cases." In essence the law applied only to parties who had been ejected from a "foreign grant" wherein the land was not eventually confirmed and granted to the original rancho claimant.

With this very brief description of the rather unstable legal aspects surrounding homesteading in early American California, the story of land settlement throughout northern Sonoma County

---

This last condition appeared again in a later law providing for the sale by the State of such public domain land as was granted to the State of California through the so-called school and desert land acts. Should any such land be sold to a settler, but actually found to be validly occupied under a prior claim, then the intended purchaser could acquire other land elsewhere of the same category. The parcel thus selected was commonly termed "lieu land." As a matter of disgraceful fact, State authorities sold some parcels of land twice or thrice, principally because of inadequate controls.

may now be discussed. For the Mexican Californians this had been the distant *Frontera del Norte*. For the restless and energetic immigrant Americans it must have appeared as truly the Promised Land.

Through the long milleniums of earth time the little green river twisted southward. In summer it sparkled on its way, gathering contributions from side streams and the oozing hillside springs. One of its most important tributaries came to be called the Valley of Tzábaco. By whom, or for what reason has long since been forgotten.

During many winter seasons, heavy rains would saturate the densely vegetated hills that were drained by the river. And then the excess of free water would flow over the land, increasing in speed and strength as it increased in volume, tearing away loose soil particles in its path. Such excessive engorging of muddy flood waters would swell the river out of its natural banks to spread over benches and small valleys where the rich soil was deposited. Then after a few days surcease from the rains, the river would recede into its natural channel, changing from churning brown to lazy green, pursuing its twisted path to the sea.

Sometime back in the misty reaches of Time the Great Spirit had created out of Red Earth the Pomo Indian People and their neighbors the Wappo. The tribelets of these aboriginal people dwelt upon the rich and pleasant flood benches and river valleys. They used several local names for the river, but mostly it seemed to have been Shabaikai, the Snake.

Food was plentiful. There were several species of acorns and berries, roots and edible plants. There were birds and waterfowl, small game animals and grasshoppers, elk, deer, squirrels, black bear and the formidable grizzly. It was a beautiful and bountiful land.

Early in the second decade of the 19th Century, the Russian fur trappers paddled their skin bidarkas up from the ocean, through a majestic colonnade of giant redwood trees. For a quarter century they trapped beaver on the river they called the Slavianka, the "pretty little Slav girl."

During the 1820's and 1830's the Mexican California government showed its concern for the intrusion of the Russians and wandering *Anglos* by establishing missions at San Rafael and Sonoma. In 1834 Pueblo Sonoma was founded. Sometimes the local Indians offered bitter resistance to the invaders of their ancient homeland. The Californians called the river San Ysidro and possibly San Sebastian. About 1843 they began to refer to it as the Russian River, *El Rio Ruso.*

Mariano Guadalupe Vallejo, a native of Monterey, first as a rising officer of the California Provincial Army, and then as a respected citizen of the new American State, was the dominant figure in the occupation and in personal acquisition of the land that became Napa and Sonoma counties.

Without question, General Vallejo was personally convinced that Alta California could not remain as a weak and isolated province of the Mexican Nation. This became especially obvious as events progressed during the 1840's. It must have been apparent to him that even without military conquest the United States would inevitably dominate the land. This would occur through the unsolicited immigration of traders and frontiersmen. It was like-wise quite evident that Vallejo showed good judgment in enlisting the assistance of worthy *Anglo* immigrants in his own business adventures, and even into his family by marriage. It does not appear that he ever had serious reason to personally regret this manner of association with representatives of a new and dynamic culture.

Physical occupation of the Russian River Valley region by ranchers acceptable to the California government was initiated as a policy in the early 1830's and then accelerated with the certainty that the dominance of Mexico was waning.

The first grant of land near present Santa Rosa was made to one Rafael Gomez who did not choose to go and live upon the wild *frontera del norte.* On the other hand, the prominent Captain John B. R. Cooper, brother-in-law of Vallejo, acquired the El Molino Rancho in 1833. The next year he undertook an unusual business venture in view of the time and place. He invested some $10,000 in the construction of the first industrial water-driven sawmill in California. This mill was erected on Mark West Creek near its junction with the Russian River at the inner edge of the vast and unexplored redwood forest.

In 1841, Maria Ignatia Lopez (Carrillo); and in 1844 Joaquin Carrillo obtained the Cabeza de Santa Rosa and Llano de Santa Rosa ranchos. They were the parents of Señora Vallejo, whose sister's husband, Henry D. Fitch became a prime occupant of the north central Santa Rosa Valley when, in 1841, he applied for and eventually obtained the Sotoyome Rancho. This small empire of 49,000 acres surrounding present Healdsburg was patented to his heirs in 1858. But not without a brawling with more than a thousand squatters which resulted in two deaths.

The rich land of the lovely Santa Rosa and Napa valleys was quite naturally coveted by many American immigrants of the 1850's. Some of them did not care what prior right of possession might be claimed under the Mexican regime. Some insisted that such alleged rights had been obtained fraudulently; and some had. The Land Claims Commission rejected nearly one-fourth of the considered claims throughout the state.

There can be no doubt that not a few of the late-coming land claimants sincerely believed they had put down roots upon the un-patented public domain when they squatted on Spanish or Mexican ranchos. And it must be remembered that many perfectly valid possessory and pre-emption homesteads on the vacant public lands were proved and patented, all in due process of law and without contention.

A topographic map of the Russian River and its adjacent drainages, between the great bend to the west through the redwood region and the narrows at the Mendocino County boundary, reveals the following general features. Mark West Creek flows west across the Santa Rosa Valley and meets the river at the bend. It was here that John Cooper constructed his sawmill. The valley at this point extends about six miles eastward to the foothills.

Ten miles to the north at Healdsburg the valley has nar-rowed to about two miles. But here the flatland has actually become the lower end of Dry Creek Valley because the Russian River has been constricted and twisted around three great loops through the low hills between Healdsburg and the Alexander Valley which lies some four airline miles to the northeast.

Dry Creek flows in from the northwest, and the Russian River follows a parallel course down the Alexander Valley. That beauti-ful valley extends some fifteen miles north to the narrows not far above the village of Cloverdale. It was named for Cyrus Alexander who settled there in 1841. He became the ranch manager for absentee grant holder Henry Fitch of Sotoyomo Rancho. A map of 1848 names this stretch of the stream the Alexander River. This was during the period when the several names for the river were giving way to the finally accepted name, Russian River.

José German Peña, more properly a resident of Pueblo Sonoma, probably began to spend most of his time in this vicinity, beginning at about the time Alexander arrived. In fact, the latter gave testimony in 1858 that Peña had tried to settle on the Sotoyomo but had moved upriver when informed that he was trespassing.

When Peña considered it expedient to formally request a grant of land he prepared a *diseño* sketch which labeled the Alexander or El Rio Ruso simply Rio Grande. Dry Creek he marked as Rio, and sketched it of a size beyond any realistic proportion. Nevertheless, this map with all of its crudeness and distortion later became a very critical exhibit in the cases at law regarding the true bounds of Señor Peña's rancho.

Citizen German Peña presented his petition to Governor Manuel Micheltorena on September 14, 1843, at Monterey. He addressed that gentleman as Señor Comandante General and Political Chief of Both Californias. Citizen Peña for his personal benefit and that of his family, asked "for the land known by the name of Tzábaca, bounded on the South by lands of Don Henrique Fitch, and on the North, East, and West by the Sierra." The request was for four square leagues of land, that is, approximately 17,000 acres. And that is essentially what Peña was granted.

It is quite important at this point to take note of several aspects of the situation. The least important is that the currently accepted name Tzábaco has appeared with several spellings, sometimes ending in letter a, and even as Tzabuco and Tzabasco.

Another peculiarity which does nothing to simplify the story of the bitter struggle that ensued to control land here is the seemingly indiscriminate placement of the Tzábaco in either Mendocino or Sonoma counties. This came about because the original 1850 boundary between these counties was the Russian River itself, from the mouth to some indeterminate point near present Hopland. Prior to 1855 any settler on the north or west side of the river would, in fact, have been in Mendocino County. After that he could presume he was not, because the legal boundary was then changed. It became a straight line from the ocean a mile above Fort Ross, thence northeasterly to some mountain peak northwest of Clear Lake. Fortunately for this case, the fact that Mendocino was only

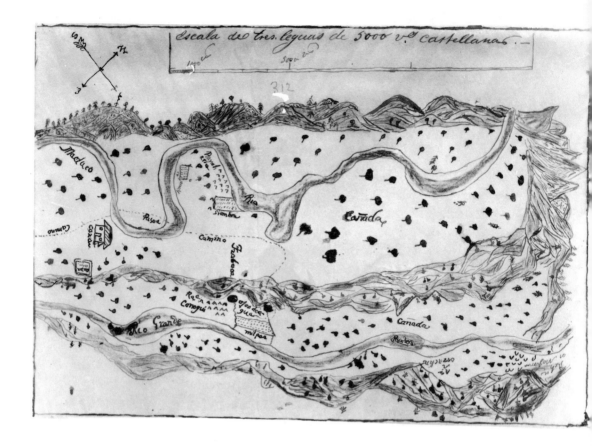

## THE DISEÑO OF RANCHO TZÁBACO

On September 25, 1843, José German Peña petitioned Governor Micheltorena for a grant of four (square) leagues, about 17,000 acres, on vacant land "known by the name of Tzabaca," north of the lands of Enrique Fitch. The Tzabaca was present Dry Creek Valley in Sonoma County. That name appears to be crudely scribed vertically near the **camino** (road) at the map center.

The difficulty of identifying or delineating a precise land area from either the **diseño** sketch or the written description is obvious. Even the carefully prepared map scale is misleading as written. The bar is correct: one league of approximately 2.5 miles equalled 5000 Castillian **varas** (of about 33 English inches each). It made no particular difference in this case. Nothing was measured or plotted to scale. Exact land boundaries were not of that much concern at the place and time.

"Rio Grande" on the map is the Russian River and "Rio" is Dry Creek. Peña could have selected several names other than Rio Grande for the river. Consider the circling mountains shown in vertical profile. Southwesterly is the open Dry Creek Valley toward Healdsburg. Conifers are shown on the mountains and presumably oaks in the **Cañadas.**

Note the river island marked "Pescadero," probably because Indians constructed gill net dams there. The Wappo People had been here for centuries where they had pushed a wedge cross the river into Pomo country. Indian villages or **rancherias** are shown by inverted "v" symbols.

A **siembra** grain field is shown on the Dry Creek side, and a corn field or **milpas,** along the Russian River. Between corn field and hills is scrawled "ojo de a-gua." This was the flowing spring of critical witness testimony of 1858. No structure is evident at this place on this map. On the Dry Creek side is marked two structures, the Peña adobe "casa." That adobe still stands, about one mile south of Couzzens Corner on the Phillips Ranch.

Along the Russian River, presumably near the flowing spring, settlers came in the 1850's. A store and a post office were constructed. Eventually came a railroad. The growing community came to be called Geyserville.

— California State Archives

a paper county from 1850 to 1859 caused all official business affairs to be conducted by the local government of the County of Sonoma until the latter year.

Also among the peculiarities of lesser importance was the common misspelling of the name of the principal family. Many documents, and especially court records, spelled the name Pina.

In retrospect it is not unreasonable to comment that no rancho land description at all in this case might have been more helpful in the final determination of its approved bounds. The one firm side, upon which so much was later hinged, was the known boundary of the Fitch claim on the south. Actually, this line ran due northeast and southwest, not east and west.

The land known as Tzábaco was bounded on all other sides by the sierra, said the description. And rather obviously the *diseño* is intended to indicate just that. A sierra is a saw-toothed mountain range. Whatever the term might have meant to Peña and his successors, the meandering southwestern boundary of Tzábaco eventually was set precisely where the flat Dry Creek Valley meets the foothills. On the northeast side the boundary was later calculated in the Surveyor-General's Office. This was done simply to gain additional land area. That line was stretched across the drainages of the brushy hills about midway between their summit and the river. Obviously then, the original written description for the exterior limits of more than three-fourths of this rancho actually contained nothing of value. Yet a basic rule in the establishment or reestablishment of land boundaries calls for the acceptance of physical monuments or objects as superior to recorded distances and directions.

The fact was, of course, that the hill land had almost no material value when the grant was requested. And no one built line fences to limit the wandering of the wild range cattle. Periodic rodeos among neighbors took care of intermingled stock.

It would seem that, next to the rather solid Sotoyomo Grant boundary line, the most important element of the description should have been the meaning of the words, "the land known by the name of Tzabaca."

German Peña died in 1847. The hearing before the Land Claims Commission, which led to confirmation of the grant to the heirs, was conducted between March of 1852 and 1855. Mariano G. Vallejo appeared as one important witness. On January 30, 1854, the General testified that he knew the place well and the people involved. He specifically referred to Dry Creek as "the Tzábaco." Said he, "The valley described on the map as the Rio Grande lying northeast of said Rancho, is not included in it . . . the boundary running along the inner range of hills. . . . The rancho extends from hill to hill . . . " on each side of Tzábaco Creek. Vallejo further testified that the brothers and sister of deceased German Peña were currently in possession and residing on said Rancho.

The date of Vallejo's testimony should be noted. This was three years following the 1851 marriage of his daughter Epifania to Captain John B. Frisbie, and four years prior to the purchase by Frisbie of the Peña holdings. In a later case at law, an attorney representing Frisbie against alleged squatters intimated rather strongly that Vallejo had given his testimony because he had personal designs upon the Russian River property. Such a thing hardly seems possible in 1854 when that land was already subject to earlier claims, and the new American government was in control. Obviously, his testimony was contrary to his son-in-law's later interest.

In September of 1853, Deputy Land Surveyor T. H. Whitacre was working at sectionizing the rugged country adjacent to Dry Creek Valley on the west. He entered in his official notes: "Dry Cr Valley is six or seven miles long and about 60 ch[ains] wide, owned and occuppied by the Penas. . . " He made no record of other settlers or squatters. It is most unlikely that any such occupants were present, and certainly not without permission of the Peña family. This portion of Dry Creek Valley was never sectionized because it was a recognized Mexican grant and its western boundary was firmly established at this date.

It also appears that two of the three judges on the Land Claims Commission went upon the land and made a note of June 26, 1855 that the rancho grant was "located in the Valley through which flows the stream known by the name of Tzabaca," and that the said area was situated in the County of Mendocino.

Deputy Surveyor Whitacre extended his survey work for the purpose of establishing section corners on both sides of the Russian River over the hills from the Peñas. This he did in October of 1853, under contract with and instructions from Surveyor-General John Hays.

The early date and the course of the survey indicate beyond any doubt that Hays deemed the Alexander Valley above Sotoyome Rancho to be public land in need of official government monuments. This would permit settlers to describe and patent their claims.

Beginning at an established point on the line between Townships 9 and 10 North, about a half-mile north of present Lytton, Whitacre and his two chainmen proceeded north. They reached the river at two miles and set a section corner. Then they zigzagged north and west, setting quarter-corners at each half mile and section corners at each 80 chain mile.[24]

---

[24]There are 66 feet in one chain and 80 chains in one mile. Whitacre's men were literally dragging a Gunter's chain composed of 100 links of stiff wire. Each link would then be 7.92 inches in length.

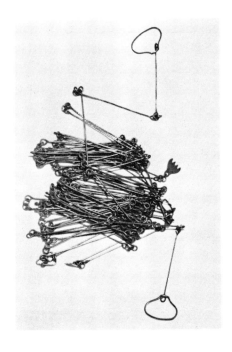

1870 Transit

Gunter's chain owned by the State Department of Parks and Recreation, Sacramento. This chain was found in old Bodie. Tags indicate number of links, i.e., 10, 20, etc. This chain is 101 links long, possibly to allow slope adjustments.

There was a simple reason for the zig-zag course. Surveyor-General King had warned against just such possible frustrations. In this place, geography had failed to cooperate with the public land subdivision system. The river and mountains, and therefore the land ownership patterns, assumed a northwesterly-southeasterly attitude.

Whitacre could have left a fascinating story of Indian villages and the varied landscape he observed along the course of his survey. Unfortunately, the inadequate government reimbursement for many contract surveys in mountainous land later came to be recognized as the cause of much poor and fraudulent work. There is no reason to believe such a thing occurred here. Yet Whitacre had to push along and his notes are minimal. As required, he made a record of the quality of soil and the general nature of the vegetation through which he passed.

Two cultural features should have been recorded if they appeared. These were structures and roads. The dearth of such notations in these survey notes made in the vicinity of present Geyserville is worthy of attention. The time was mid-October of 1853. Whitacre and party had set the southeast corner of Section 18, Township 10 North, Range 9 West. Running west to create a south boundary for Section 18, the surveyors were forced to wade or swim the Russian River before proceeding two chains. At one-half mile, in "first quality soil" a quarter-section stake was set. This must have been several hundred feet southeast of the present crossing of Highway 128, or Old Calistoga Road, over the railroad track on the south of Geyserville.

Proceeding due west, through the present business district, climbing about 530 feet farther west they set the important southwest corner of Section 18 on the Range line. Then they started north, angling across the face of the hills.

After a measured one-fourth mile the party again reached the "foot of the mountain." But back five chains on the hillside, Surveyor Whitacre could turn his compass due east directly toward "Couzens house," 8 chains distant.[25]

---

[25]Obed E. Bosworth, merchant of Geyserville, states (letter to author 8 June 1970): "The same year that Ely settled on his ranch (1851) Davenport Cozzens settled on the east side of the Main Road immediately north of the present Christian Church, and after a couple of years moved almost directly across the River and was living there when Allen C. Kilgore, my grandfather, settled next to him in 1857." Five years after the survey the site of Cozzens' house was claimed by John Clar.

Prominent structures would naturally be recorded in a public survey of this nature. This was because they could be expected to endure for many years as physical monuments which could be found and identified with relative ease. The point of interest in this case it that no other structure was mentioned by Whitacre until he noted Tenham's house, across the river and about three miles upstream.

No adobe structure belonging to Peña and no flowing spring or corn field was noted, and there was then no recorded evidence of the presence of Doctor Elisha Ely upon the ground in the vicinity of present Geyserville.

As mentioned, it was also important that surveyors in wild land note the roads they crossed. In this case it is difficult to assume other than that Whitacre was not impressed by the trail which soon became a recognized public road and eventually the Redwood Highway. He obviously crossed its course twice while establishing the south and west lines of Section 18. Probably it appeared as just another foot trail used by animals and men.

Evidence thus far presented in respect to the exclusion of the Alexander Valley from Tzábaco Rancho has been substantial. It was not until the critical year of 1858 that contrary evidence favorable to the four heirs of José German Peña was brought forth. That testimony will be revealed in its chronological order so that the position of the growing colony of settlers along the Russian River can be more properly appreciated.

———

Down on the Sotoyome Rancho the number of squatters upon the land legally claimed by the successors to Henry Fitch were declared to exceed 2000 angry men. Many squatter families were cultivating the land and cutting the timber. Hardly a shadow of legal justification could have been found to favor their position. Yet they were determined to stay. And it appears that no sheriff's posse had the force or the stomach to add further blood to the two deaths already mentioned.

The *Journal* of the California Senate of March 7, 1856, (page 438) contains an interesting commentary on the problem in this part of the State. It was indicated earlier that this period produced the zenith of squatter power in the State Legislature.

The *Journal* entry was titled, "Memorial of farmers and actual settlers of Sonoma County, praying for prompt passage of law to protect persons making permanent improvements on lands, in the belief that the same were pre-emptable, and showing depression of farming interests as the result of a lack of such protection."

The Memorial was represented by one Thomas A. Hylton and 275 others. It went on to explain that every man engaged in agricultural pursuits was vitally in need of prompt aid and protection. "To you, then, fellow citizens whom we have elevated to a high position and honor, we turn for this security, strong in the belief that any just man knows it to be but fair and reasonable— every true man feels friendly to a measure so necessary and so right."

Fortunately, the one man who did most to settle this thorny issue felt impelled to write his autobiography in 1887. This he titled, *Life and Adventures of Colonel L. A. Norton.* As an attorney who chose Healdsburg for his future home, he was hired by Dr. L. C. Frisbie of Vallejo to evict the squatters from Sotoyome Rancho. With great personal courage, a developing reputation for personal honesty and integrity, and such rough treatment as the burning of squatter homes, he actually quieted the situation. His ultimate solution came through granting title to the squatters under firm but reasonable terms. Norton said he arrived on the ground in the summer of 1858. Presumably the miracle he claims to have worked took place during the following several years.

The subjects of Sotoyome Rancho and Colonel Norton may now be set aside while the conditions of settlement farther north are considered.

Two other rancho requests were granted by the Mexican Governor on the northern border of the Tzábaco. One was the Casalamayome of nearly 28,000 acres, claimed by Eugenio Montenegro in 1844. Exactly 30 years elapsed before a patent was obtained for this rancho. Most of the area consisted of steep hills of grass and brush. The steam vents called geysers were within this claim. Probably a dearth of arable land saved this Mexican rancho from an intrusion of squatters.

The bulk of the Alexander Valley above Tzábaco was embraced by the Rancho Rincon de Musalacon. Francisco Berreyessa requested this land in 1846. Near the center of this 9000 acre grant the town of Clover Dale began to develop. Farther north, in much more isolated country, Fernando Feliz in 1844 requested

the 18,000 acre Sanel Rancho. This area surrounds present Hopland. No wagon road approached it from the south until probably as late as 1860.

The squatter tide seems to have lost its violent impact before it reached this far north. More important, the land ownership was undoubtedly firm and recognized, as it seems to have been in upper Dry Creek Valley.

There was, of course, always the small advance guard among the pioneer *Anglos* drifting out into the little known public domain. There were, for example, such men as Hiram Willits and the Potter brothers who left their names on the landscape at the headwaters of the Russian River. Though little has been recorded of them and their kind, it can be assumed that they possessed some personal quality which made them acceptable to the great number of primitive Indians among whom they chose to live.

The first *Anglo* settler or squatter to stop and remain on the west side of the Russian River in the vicinity of present Geyserville is said to have been Dr. Elisha Ely. This occurred in 1851, ten years after German Peña began to develop a cattle ranch there. Lacking contrary evidence it can be assumed that there was no serious dispute regarding the earliest American settlement on the Russian River side.

Archibald C. Godwin is supposed to have constructed the first store in the vicinity in 1854. So there must have been a growing community of settlers by that time, notwithstanding Whitacre's failure to note them a year earlier. Godwin acquired the hot air geysers, which he intended to promote as a natural attraction. Very possibly, this commercial interest in the geysers caused him to instigate and press the misleading name Geyserville on the Russian River community of settlers. Yet, one rare map of 1857 shows the name Godwin as a single indication of settlement in that vicinity.[26]

Most of the later sightseers traveled to the geysers by horse stage from Cloverdale. Geyserville, or more properly Clairville Station, became the steam train terminus for parties bound for another popular spa, namely, Skaggs Springs.

There was another map compiled in 1857. This one came from the Office of U. S. Surveyor-General. Its principal purpose was

---

[26]At Bancroft Library; Britton and Rey Map of Cal., 1857, G.H. Goddard, C.E. Godwin became a colonel in the Union Army and lost his life in battle. The "discoverer" of the geyser area was William B. Elliot in 1847, not Godwin as sometimes reported.

to show the location of confirmed Spanish and Mexican grant lands. The Tzábaco Rancho was not indicated on this map. The grant had been confirmed by the Lands Commission in 1855 and by the District Court in April of 1857. However, the fact remained that right of possession was still under serious contention. Or more specifically, the land boundaries of Tzábaco were in serious dispute.

A single place name marked this isolated portion of California. The name on the map was CLARVILLE.

What induced the Clar family to move to the northern frontier and attempt to become farmers? This would seem to have been a profession for which neither man nor wife were psychologically or technically qualified. The need to move and the opportunity to acquire land must have been the inducement. John had plenty of forewarning that he would be removed from the General Land Office. It can also be assumed that few individuals of that time possessed a greater accumulation of knowledge in respect to the status and relative agricultural quality of available public land. Both he and his close friend Jack Hays must still have believed that the Alexander Valley between Sotoyome and Casalamayome ranchos was public domain open to homesteaders.

Book P of Possessory Claims in the Office of the Recorder of Sonoma County contains a filing by John Clar on October 23, 1857. The claimant declared that he had entered upon and was in possession of a parcel of land comprising 160 acres. He said the land was in Township 10 North, Range 9 West according to the U. S. Survey.

The claim was a square, with four sides each one-half mile in length. The starting point was a tree marked J C, "at the foot of the hill range lying near the right [looking downstream] bank of the Russian River." Southeasterly a half-mile "along the foot of said hill range" another tree was marked J C & C F. The latter initial represented the claimant Charles Fisk. The two then used a common boundary which ran northeasterly a half-mile to the bank of the Russian River. It is to be noted that the Godwin Ranch adjoined the Clar Ranch along the northwest side, according to the description.

In National Archives is a copy of a letter from the Commissioner of the General Land Office in Washington to John Clar, Esquire. It was dated March 2, 1858, and was addressed to Geyserville, Sonoma County. The letter referred to back pay. Its historical significance rests in confirming the subject's former

employment status, the name of his mailing address at the date of transmittal, and the fact that he was on the ground and not an absentee claimant.

This matter of absenteeism is open to some question, as evidenced by the document of record now introduced as the next step in the elusive history of one pioneer family upon the virgin land. The exhibit is deposited in the California State Achives. It represents part of the record of a case at law.

On the 15th day of April, A. D. 1858, the Sheriff of the County of Sonoma certified that he served upon one James M. Bradford a summons, in the town of Geyserville. The service involved the complaint of John Clar, also a citizen of Sonoma County, who alleged a breach of contract on the part of defendant Bradford. The sheriff requested for his service, one dollar; and for travel of 25 miles, $7.50.

Plaintiff Clar declared in the formal complaint that on the 5th day of August, 1857, he and Bradford had entered into a written agreement. Clar had agreed to furnish the sum of $1800. This money Bradford had promised "to lay out and invest in stock and farming utensils to be placed and used upon a certain farm of the plaintiff . . . described as follows: bounded by the Russian River, the hills on the south, the Rancho of Dr. Ely on the Westward and the claim formerly held by R. Harrison on the Eastward, containing about one hundred and sixty acres."[27]

This exhibit immediately introduces several interesting and perplexing elements. The date of the contract predates Clar's departure from the Land Office by three months. Possibly that explains why a resident ranch manager was sought for a claim not yet filed upon. But the land description varies in this summons of April 1858 from the possessory claim of October 1857 in one peculiar respect. In the claim, the neighbor to the north was Godwin, and on the south Fisk. Now Dr. Ely is set to the north, and

---

[27]Richard Harrison can be found in Mendocino County history as a grantee of the first deed of record when that county began to function in 1859. He is also said to have been the first judge to sit in that county. He was an attorney who handled the estate of members of the Peña family. It would be most interesting to know if he deserted the Geyserville settlement as a claimant because he knew the Peña heirs would win their contest. Richard appears frequently in land exchange records of Sonoma County, as does his brother Thomas. The latter operated a store in Geyserville in 1864 according to his granddaughter Mrs. Nancy Henshall of San Francisco.

the former claim of Harrison to the south. That peculiarity seems to have an unusual but logical solution which will be proposed with the next exhibit.

In the complaint Clar went on to declare that Bradford had agreed to sow seed, to purchase and care for livestock and farming equipment for a period of two years. The profit arising from the farming venture was to be shared equally. Plaintiff had made the payment in cash as agreed upon. But the defendant "has wholly failed and neglected . . . these duties . . . and instead of investing said sum . . . took and appropriated sixteen hundred dollars thereof . . . to his own use and benefit." The defendant further was alleged to have cut and sold hay to the value of $300, to have been incompetent, and to have abandoned the property about the first of March, 1858. In brief, plaintiff sought to recover damages to the extent of one thousand dollars in cash.

On April 24, an attorney for Bradford filed a demurrer, claiming the complaint did not state facts sufficient to constitute a cause of action.

There apparently being no further known record of this case at law in the files of the County of Sonoma, we rest the case of Clar versus Bradford without editorial opinion.

The first days of March 1858, as mentioned in the letter from Washington and this lawsuit, might indicate the physical arrival of the Clar family in the Geyserville vicinity. The next document of record lends considerable weight to that theory.

In the County Recorder's Book 7 of Deeds the following deed of June 9, 1858, may be read. One Asahel Whitney, of the County of Sonoma, "for and in consideration of the friendship and esteem I have for Angèle Clar, wife of John Clar of Sonoma County, do hereby donate and give to said Angèle Clar . . . the following described parcel of ground . . . a tract of land to the extent of about six acres together with two houses situated thereon, built by Richard Harrison and John Clar, respectively, with all their tenements and fences appertaining thereto, also a spring of water . . . " And the said Angéle Clar was to have a right-of-way from the premises to the Public Road.

The spring was apparently flowing in a gully or ravine and it was about 300 yards distant southwesterly from the houses. This raises the tantilizing question as to whether the flowing spring was the *ojo de agua* marked on the Tzábaco *diseño* and which

played such an important part in testimony before the Land Claims Commission at the very time this deed was recorded.

A. C. Godwin and W. W. Riddleton were witnesses to the signature of Whitney. The deed was dated about six weeks prior to the birth of Madame Clar's second son, which occurred in San Francisco in late July of 1858."[28]

There was more to this brief deed, which already contains several puzzles. Why had the transfer of property been made to a woman, especially one living with her lawful husband? And why had her husband built a house which was now deeded to her? The concluding description appears to further complicate the enigma, but it actually provides the solution. The six acres parcel of land was stated to be a "part of what was formerly known as the claim of Richard Harrison, bounded by the Rancho formerly claimed by A. C. Godwin on the northwest and by the claim of Charles Fisk on the southeast, by the Russian River on the northeast and the hills on the southwest."

That is familiar language. Godwin and Fisk properties were in the same relative position to the Clar possessory claim. In this deed Harrison was a "former claimant" and Whitney the current claimant on this piece of property bearing the same relationship to Godwin and Fisk properties.

In the lawsuit Clar said he was bounded by the *former* claim of Harrison on the eastward, that is the southeast. Obviously then, Clar had simply moved upriver, onto what he described as Godwin's Ranch in the description of his possessory claim in October 1857. In the later sale deed for this property this supposition is supported. The description there says his land was "formerly the land of Archi-

---

[2] This son was the writer's father. He remembered that his mother had told him the trip to San Francisco required three days, probably with stage night stops at Santa Rosa and Petaluma. The stage terminal and embarcadero, about six miles from Petaluma, was named Donahue. From that important salt water port a rather elegant paddle-wheel steamer made thrice-weekly runs to San Francisco. It happened that the stage driver on this trip was a remarkable frontiersman and Mexican War veteran named John Washington Bagley. He was a founder of the town of Guerneville and is buried there.

This entire Geyserville venture quite naturally assumed little importance in the memory of John Clar's sons, since the oldest was less than four years when they departed. There was in this writer's family a precious little watertight basket said to have been presented to Madame Clar by friendly Wappo women. It was stolen about 1925. There was also a mild joke in the family that this child Ivon, or Jack, was really an Indian changeling baby from Clarville, because of his retiring disposition. He actually possessed a great empathy for Indians and spent the winter of 1880 in the Hoopa Valley.

bald C. Godwin." The reason for Clar having built a house where he did, and of Whitney's transfer of it without a money consideration is now clear.

These people seem to have been making very firm business deals. Nevertheless, no patent of land transfer from the State or Federal governments was on record. John Clar had filed on his limit of 160 acres. No need to jeopardize that claim with an additional recorded deed in his name to six acres, even though it involved his own house.

Several important events of 1858 moved the Tzábaco Rancho case to a final decision but not the conclusion of the question of ownership and possession. These events embraced the purchase of Peña interests by John B. Frisbie; surveys by the Surveyor-General to establish the true boundary of the Tzábaco; and new and critical testimony by witnesses who favored Frisbie.

Captain John B. Frisbie was an officer in the military government of American California when he was billeted at Pueblo Sonoma in 1847. He was then 24 years of age and obviously ambitious. He was a lawyer who soon left the army to run for lieutenant governor. Both John and his brother Dr. L. C. Frisbie married daughters of General Vallejo. John became a prominent banker and business man in Vallejo City, and eventually a member of the State Legislature. In 1880, John Frisbie acquired from the three Peña brothers their interest to Rancho de Tzábaco for $20,000 "lawful money." In the same month sister Clara Peña Fitch sold her share to José Luco, who transferred that undivided share six months later to Frisbie for $16,000. Then a year later Frisbie sold a half interest to attorney W. H. Patterson of San Francisco without profit. The battle for land control was now joined in earnest.

It has been stated heretofore that the U. S. District Court had presumably settled the question of ownership and boundaries of Tzábaco Rancho in 1857 in favor of Peña heirs. Yet in some way the issue must have been kept alive. Possibly John C. Hays, through both personal opinion and his position of official responsibility as U. S. Surveyor-General would not yield to what he believed to be an erroneous judgment. With the dissolution of the Land Claims Commission, jurisdiction now was vested in that office.

At any rate, Surveyor-General Mandeville sent Deputy Surveyor C. C. Tracy upon the ground in April of 1858 to survey and fix the northern and eastern boundary of the Mexican grant. In

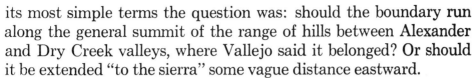

its most simple terms the question was: should the boundary run along the general summit of the range of hills between Alexander and Dry Creek valleys, where Vallejo said it belonged? Or should it be extended "to the sierra" some vague distance eastward.

Tracy placed his lines essentially as they are accepted today. His survey embraced about 15,000 acres including, of course, the Geyserville area.

Colonel Norton says at page 337 of his *Life and Adventures*:

> I was aware that about a month before my arrival in Healdsburg, a mob had taken and destroyed the field notes of Surveyor-General Tracy, gave him four hours to leave or hang, and that a like mob had chased Dr. L. C. Frisbie; he only escaping by being mounted on a fast horse . . .

The situation was certainly unpleasant regardless of the precise accuracy of Norton's version. On December 20, 1860, a group of settlers of the Geyserville community entered suit against Frisbie and Patterson, demanding that the defendants cease bothering the honest and legitimate settlers upon the public lands. They declared that their homes were situated exclusively and entirely in the Valley of the Russian River and not the land known as Tzábaco Valley.[29]

For the moment, the primary subject is the land surveys conducted in 1858. The following excerpt from trial records reveals what the settlers thought of the Tracy survey. (The asserted date is clearly erroneous).

> On or about        day of June 1859 the alleged plaintiffs [Frisbie and Patterson] conspired with one C. C. Tracy, then acting U. S. Deputy Surveyor and did thereby fraudulently and wrongfully procure a pretended survey and plat purporting to be the land confirmed to J. Jesus Pena, Antonio Pena and other heirs. Because of said fraudulent and wrongful survey, on the 19th day of May, A. D. 1860 . . . the United States instituted their action against said defendants.

On July 7, 1858, John C. Hays came upon the rancho to begin his survey. It is interesting that all of his notes refer to this as being in the County of Mendocino, while Tracy, three months earlier,

---

[29]Cal. State Archives, Superior Court Records Group, Ely et al versus Frisbie et al, 1861, case 5385; and Frisbie, et al versus Ely et al, 1861, Case 1625. The individual number of settlers represented in each lawsuit cannot be stated with accuracy because of the dubious status of some names. Probably 36; not counting those ubiquitous scofflaws John Doe and Richard Roe, and their lesser known associates, Cotton Mather, Captain Cuttle, Peregrine Pickle, John Quirk, Richard Barleycorn and Littleback Titmouse.

assumed that he was working in Sonoma County. It would be of much more interest to know if Hays paid a visit to his old associate of the Oakland Purchase and the Land Office, Rancher John Clar. There is no record of Hays having entered the Russian River Valley. He took the northeastern line of Tzábaco Rancho generally along the wandering height of land between the two valleys.

Between August 24 and October 1st, 1858, depositions were made before a notary public in San Francisco by five men in respect to the commonly recognized boundary of the Tzábaco Rancho. This action was clearly at the instigation of attorneys for Frisbie and Patterson. And the procedure was promptly objected to by attorneys for Ely et al, on the grounds that the hearing should have been held by the Surveyor-General; that they had never received notice that this was to be a public hearing; and that one deponent, Jesus Peña was an heir and therefore not a qualified witness.[30]

Peña said he presently lived on Dry Creek and had been in the region since 1841. His brother had built a house over on the river side in 1842 near the spring shown on the *diseño*, and had cultivated the land and planted grapes. He further deposed that a house had also been built across the Russian River on the east side.

Jasper O'Farrel and Jacob Lesse testified that they were present on the ground at the juridical ritual of taking possession of Sotoyome Rancho. German Peña was also present and the subject of the Tzábaco boundaries was discussed in detail. All present agreed that the ranchos were adjoining along a common line.

John Knight testified that he had come to the Sonoma country in 1841. He had gone to the Russian River area in 1852, he said, and tried to purchase land from the Peña family but apparently could not. He further stated that Peña was living at the place marked *ojo de agua*, where there were enclosed fields and grapes. José German Peña had died in 1847, as already mentioned.

Cyrus Alexander testified that he came to California in 1841 and lived eight miles from the Peña Ranch. He declared that a house was built at the spring in 1843 and that fields were cultivated there and also across the river.

This in essence was the strong testimony refuting principally the testimony of General Vallejo. That testimony had been given

---

[30]Microfilm copy of documents in Bancroft Library file C-I-100; General Land Office, Docket 167, Tzábaco Rancho.

four years earlier and without serious challenge before the Land Claims Commission.

John Frisbie undoubtedly knew his way around Washington and he went there, probably in early 1861. He is credited with having had considerable impact in respect to giving more weight to the rights of rancho claimants. The entire issue was, of course, much broader than this one case. At this time General Vallejo was much involved in trying to rescue for himself the Soscol grant near Napa City.

Senator Gwin seems to have injected himself into the Tzábaco case by writing to Land Commissioner Hendricks asking that no final decision be made on the case until Frisbie's attorney could be heard.

President Buchanan also wrote Hendricks. By a letter of June 25, 1859, he introduced his "valued friend" from Pennsylvania, one Henry S. McGraw. McGraw apparently came west and scrutinized all documents if not the actual land. He favored the Tracy survey. In the same month Mandeville in San Francisco advised Hendricks that he was personally in agreement with the Tracy report.

The position of the honest and industrious settlers at Clarville-Geyserville became even more uncomfortable when, in the suit of ejectment involving Frisbie et al versus Ely et al, the plaintiffs won a judgment of $20,000 against the settlers as well as orders for them to vacate the land.

But the settlers still insisted that the powerful machinery of the law had dealt with them dishonestly and unjustly. They refused to move and defied the local law enforcement officials.

Meanwhile, a half dozen miles south, in the village of Healdsburg, the fame of tough lawyer and local defender of the Union cause, Colonel L. A. Norton, was growing apace. Informer friends assured Norton that he would be assassinated should he set foot on the newly delineated Russian River area of the Tzábaco Rancho.

Frisbie and Patterson were advised by the Sheriff of Sonoma County to hire Norton to settle this confrontation. This they did and Norton agreed, providing he alone could make final and binding settlements on his own terms. And this is what transpired.

Norton described in considerable detail how he undertook and accomplished this task. Unfortunately, he neglected to establish the date he drove his buggy to the first settler's cabin across the Tzábaco line. Probably it was in 1863 or 1864. Old Captain Vessor was working in his yard when his ancient eyes focused on the visitor and recognized him as the terrible lawyer Norton. Norton aimed a bottle of whiskey at the old man, and then applied its soothing power to restore the ancient nerves.

Norton then took Vessor as a hostage to the claim of Dr. Elisha Ely. Norton recognized Ely as the intelligent and reasonable leader in this settler, or squatter, defiance. Ely was naturally also taken by surprise, but he discussed the matter and came to an agreement with Norton.

The latter informed Ely that he knew the legal owners were demanding too high a price for the land, and that the settlers could not raise the cash to meet the penalty set by the court. He wished to see every man own his own home. He also knew that if these people were driven from theirs, they would go to the hills and continue to fight.

Ely was very surprised, but he had heard that Norton was a man of his word. He agreed to alert all of the settlers on the following Thursday, when Norton would return. Then all together they would set a reasonable value for each farm. This was accomplished. Norton wrote: "as a result every man purchased his farm within the ensuing six weeks, paying one-fourth down and getting three years to pay the balance, at one percent interest . . . and thus ended the squatter war that had kept up for over seven years in the northern portion of this country. I must say in justification of these men that most of them, in my judgment, were honest in their convictions that the claimants had no title to the land, or if they had a title it was fraudulent."

The last known documentation involving the personal association of John Clar's family and Geyserville may be found in Sonoma County Book 8 of Deeds. Therein, a handwritten indenture of several pages reveals that on January 31, 1859, John and Angèle Clar of the County of Sonoma did sell and in every way divest themselves of a certain parcel or piece of land. Very strangely, the word Sonoma was crossed out and Mendocino inserted as the proper county of the State of California.

The land being sold was known as "Clar Ranch." It embraced approximately 160 acres, except for about two acres with appurtenances thereon heretofore sold to Richard Harrison. Perhaps that sale involved a return of Harrison's house. However, the deed declared that this Clar Ranch had formerly been the land of A. C. Godwin. It was distant eight miles northwesterly from the town of Healdsburg and bounded by the river on the northeast, the hills on the southwest, the land of Elisha Ely on the northwest, and the land of Asahel Whitney on the southeast. This land "comprised the greater portion of the Southwest quarter of Section 18, Township 10 North and Range 9 West." Why these land transactions were not tied by bearing and distance to one of the corners established by Surveyor Whitacre is somewhat of a mystery.

At any rate, Robert and David Campbell purchased the Clar Ranch for $2000 lawful money of the United States. As was customary, Angèle Clar was taken aside by the Recorder to assure that official that she understood the transaction and was not signing the deed through fear or compulsion of her husband.

The Clars must certainly have returned to San Francisco with sons aged one and three years, respectively.

Why their name was associated with the pleasant little community is not known. Certainly, the professor was a dignified scholar and his Parisian wife was an elegant and beautiful lady. Their residence was also at the center of the growing community.

Based on the accepted southeastern boundary of the former property of Dr. Elisha Ely where it crosses the Redwood Highway the location of the Clar claims can be reasonably reconstructed.[31]

The present Geyserville High School would seem to have been where the original and later claims met. That is, the first parcel extended south a half-mile to embrace the present business district. The second extended up the highway a half-mile to the little Wood Creek drainage. Probably the site of the flowing spring and the houses deeded to Angèle Clar in 1858 can never be precisely relocated. It is remembered, however, that Wood Creek itself was once a living stream which degenerated into a virtual bog on the flood plain above the river.

In further respect to the community itself, an historian of 1880 wrote: "The hamlet consists of one store, one post and express office, one saloon, one hotel, one blacksmith shop. Geyserville is not so much a place as it is these establishments." At this particular time the post office name was officially spelled Clairville.

---

[31]Obed Bosworth of Geyserville, in 1970, described the Ely south line as being on the north side of the highway culvert through which flows Wood Creek, approximately 1800 feet southeast of the junction of Redwood Highway and Canyon Road. Bosworth also recollected that "the Town of Clarville, before the days of the railroad, was located a good deal to the north of the present town, most of it being from the present High School to the present Elementary School."

It was not changed to "Guyserville" until March 3, 1887. In 1861 the Wells Fargo Directory said to direct freight and parcels to Clareville.[32]

A scrutiny of the origin of town names and other place names often reveals many curiosities. This lovely community, now bearing a name neither highly euphonious nor geographically accurate, could just as well have become known as Godwin, or Ely, or even a twisted version of Clarville.

---

[32]**History of Sonoma County**, Alley Bowen pub., S. F. 1880.
Walter N. Frickstad in **A Century of Post Offices** gives the above date for Guyserville. A corrected spelling followed a year later. There is no question but that Geyserville was the most commonly used name for this place from the 1860's on.

An album of news clips in State Library, presumably **Santa Rosa Republican** of 1887, refers to Clairville, a town of 150 persons. In the 1950's an old store front sign on the main highway was showing "Clairville" through a deteriorating paint cover.

Looking south across Alexander Valley. Geyserville is at base of the mountains about center of the picture.

John Clar's sons
San Francisco, circa 1865
Frank Lawrence, rear
Ivon Matthew, seated
Maurice David, left
Clarence in high chair, deceased
    in childhood

# 10 Santa Barbara Interlude

During most of year 1859 it can be assumed that John Clar undertook private surveying jobs within or adjacent to San Francisco. State Archives contain a couple of letters which indicate that he sought employment for which he was more qualified than ranching. One of his recognized accomplishments was translating from Spanish to English or the opposite. These letters refer to such a task.

San Francisco, Cal., March 1st., 1859

Hon. Ferris Foreman
Secretary of State Cal.
    Sir:
    In view of your public notice of the 19th January last, I propose to translate the laws of the present Legislature into Spanish for eighty cents per folio and under the other terms contained in said notice.

I have the honor to be
Very respectfully
Your Obt. Servt.
John Clar

To Col. Ferris Foreman
Sec. of State
    Sir:
    We the undersigned will file the requisite bond for the faithful translation of the Laws of the State for 1859 into the Spanish by Capt. John Clar in case the said translation be awarded him.

Henry Hancock
Andres Pico

There were other applicants, and this one did not receive the job. Andrés Pico, incidentally, was a brother of Pío Pico, last Mexican Governor of Alta California. Andrés apparently was not overwhelmed by the aggressive *Anglo* newcomers. He seems to have been quite active in the business affairs of the San Francisco Bay region.

The next known episode in the life of the Clar family involves their move to the little Spanish village of Santa Barbara, California. Just why they went there is not known, but it is likely that the powerful de la Guerra family made some inducement to the free lance surveyor. It is certain that they were in Santa Barbara in the year 1860 with their two children. Very likely they left San Francisco in mid-1859.

The census of 1860 reveals that there were 2,351 people in the City of Santa Barbara, of which 127 were Indians. The whites were certainly mostly descendants of the old *Californios*. The county at that time included all of present Ventura County and boasted a total of 3,543 souls.

In the election of November 6, 1860, John Clar was elected Superintendent of Schools for Santa Barbara County. There were 1,621 students at that time, undoubtedly most of them at the county seat attending four adobe schools, and most of them speaking Spanish more fluently than English.

State records are completely silent on the tour of duty of this Superintendent of schools. County Supervisor's minutes reveal the certain fact of his election, however. And Society of California Pioneers archives contain what is apparently a copy of another minute order. On May 20th, 1861, at a Special Session the County Board of Supervisors:

> Ordered that John Clar be and is hereby appointed Justice of the peace in and for the 2nd Township of this County.

The record of the appointee's oath of office, taken two days later, is also noted.

The Santa Barbara *Daily Press* of May 3, 1884, more than 20 years after the departure of the Clar family, gave an indication of how the San Franciscans were received in the lovely southern community. After quoting an Oakland paper in respect to the death of John Clar, the *Press* continued:

> "Mr. Clar resided in this city for several years, at an early period, and was Justice of the Peace, having his office on the Plaza de la Guerra, near the City Hall. He was master of eight languages and dialects, which he spoke with fluency, and was one of the best translators in the State. His wife, who died about four years ago, was regarded by many as the most beautiful and most graceful lady in all California, and they were both highly esteemed in this community for their intelligence and social qualities."

On or about the day of the 1860 election a son Maurice was born to the Clars. His baptismal record (and that of his older brother at the same time) coupled with the June census record provide at least an official picture of the family since, regrettably, so little is known of their activities there.

In the census, the head of the family was named John, aged 48, a Professor of Mathematics who valued his personal estate at $5,000. His wife was named Angelia (so the recorder said) and there were sons Lawrence 5 years, and Ivon 2. It is interesting that the Señor reverted to his title of 15 years earlier. Very possibly he was teaching school prior to being elected Superintendent of Schools.

Then in the baptismal record five months later it is noted that Juan Clar and Ana Lesgent were the parents of sons Ivon and Maurice who were baptised on that 10th day of November 1860.[33]

In the summer of 1863 the family returned to San Francisco and found residence on Dupont Street (now Grant Avenue) near Greenwich. John was reemployed at the General Land Office as an archive clerk.

Apparently this work continued for six years when he was again dismissed.

---

[33]Ivon, of the phenomenal memory, undoubtedly remembered playing with Indian children around the Old Mission Fountain. However, he was not baptised there as he had always presumed, nor at the Presidio Chapel but rather at the long departed Our Lady of Sorrows Church at Figuroa and State streets (according to Rev. Maynard Geiger). The child very well might have yelled, "Too much water," as he claimed, without being aware that he said it in French or Spanish. He spoke little English when he entered school in San Francisco.

A sponsor at the christening was one Lena Lesgent, possibly a sister of Madame Clar, and it would seem that she must have arrived from France in mid-1860. She was not recorded in the 1860 census. There was deposited at Santa Barbara Historical Museum by this writer an envelope preserved by son Maurice, his daughter Angèle, and her daughter Angèle Beatrice (Shaw). (The original letter is not known to exist). The envelope is addressed to Madame Angèle Clar at Santa Barbara via Angleterre. The November stamp in Paris (and Boston) show no year. It must have been 1859. A faded note in French on the back says, in free translation, "I will be arriving by sea very soon. The news I bring will overwhelm you."

John Clar
November 1883

Angele Lesgent Clar
July 1877

# 11  The Old Man's Place

*I*n 1868 John Clar, aged 55, was again dismissed from his staff position at the U. S. General Land Office. Whether or not the election of Grant to the presidency was a factor cannot be said. However, it was at this time that a civil service bill began to take shape in Congress in response to the growing disgust among many substantial citizens regarding the manner of selecting federal employees on the basis of political favoritism.

In that year of 1868 the California Legislature provided for a Board of Tidelands Commissioners to survey the tidelands of San Francisco Bay. One prescribed duty was the extension of San Francisco City into the shallow waters south of Second Street. An earlier law had provided for similar work north of this point.

State Archives and two field note books in the State Lands Division reveal the fact that John Clar was hired by Chief Engineer Allardt to be a third Assistant Engineer on this project at a monthly salary of two hundred dollars. He seems to have reported for work on May 19th and remained until December 8, 1868. His name appears on the official map of extended San Francisco streets.

Chief Allardt chose to write a special letter of instructions on October 28 to Transitman Clar regarding the survey between Candlestick Rock and the San Mateo County boundary. The letter and a precise sketch which was rendered in three colors is reproduced here.

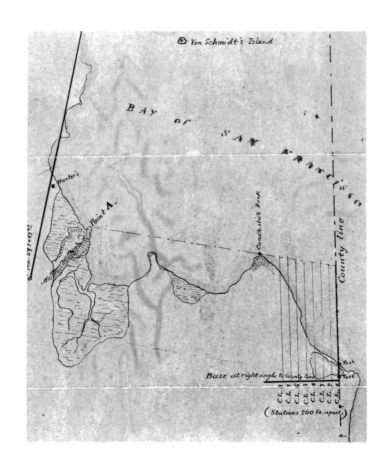

Office of Tide Land Survey.
Oct. 28~ 1868.

John Clar, Er
 3ᵈ Assist Sup.
  Dear Sir – Above sketch shows the
Sounding Lines to be run between "Candlestick Rock" and
the County line. — The boat will be brought in range with
said rock and the Point A, and then rowed ashore along
the red lines. — In running your Base, you will connect
with either monument on the County line.
  Yours
    respectfully
(Mr. Blair remains on the Island)  S. F. Allardt
      Engineer.

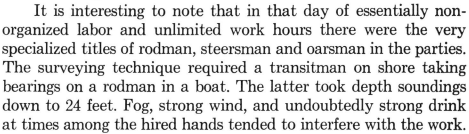

It is interesting to note that in that day of essentially non-organized labor and unlimited work hours there were the very specialized titles of rodman, steersman and oarsman in the parties. The surveying technique required a transitman on shore taking bearings on a rodman in a boat. The latter took depth soundings down to 24 feet. Fog, strong wind, and undoubtedly strong drink at times among the hired hands tended to interfere with the work.

Far out in left field from Candlestick Rock and Mr. Hunter's house is a speck of land in the bay labeled on recent maps as Shag Rock. On that island of less than one acre in size there stood a house in 1868. And the rock or island was known as Shag, Shagg, Powder, or von Schmidt's Island. Alexy W. von Schmidt had acquired title to the property by patent from the State. In 1868 this was an important transit position.

Third Engineer Clar entered in his notebook on the day of October 23rd, 1868, this personal and petulant query: "I was ready at ½ past six. What is the reason I was not taken to Shag Islet til ¼ past 9 o'clock? I know." There was no wind or fog recorded on that day.

From 1869 through 1878 city directories list Clar as a surveyor. Undoubtedly, during this period he was assisted in numerous private surveys by his brilliant, ambitious, and somewhat eccentric eldest son who was called Lawrence Frank. The youth had never received any formal schooling but was at various times an assayer, woodcarver, miner, lumberman, and teacher of telegraphy at the prominent Pacific Business College about 1880. He was also an outstanding cornetist.

At this time the family moved to 1220 Polk Street where Madame Clar operated a dry goods or "fancy goods" store. In adjoining quarters the parents lived the remainder of their lives. And here youngest son Leonce was born in 1870.

In July of 1879 John was again hired by the Land Office with the title of translator at an annual salary of $2,000. He continued in the position until his death five years later.

On April 5, 1880, Madame Clar died of "bilious cholera," the result of having eaten canned mushrooms several days earlier. John Clar was now a frail and aging man, suffering increasingly from rheumatism.

Among relic papers is one important fragment of what appears to have been intended as a personal letter. In a failing hand the writer notes with regret that:

> Lawrence Frank with solid talents is frittering away in this little shop. . . . Yet without him I do not know how I could have got along. . . . Need I say anything about her — that heavenly messenger whom the Supreme Being thought proper for awhile to allot to us for my consolation, and take away to my utter desolation. True, there is no death. But shall we ever meet those angelic creations that made earth a paradise? I hope so.

There remains now only the story of two letters. Although they were written nearly two years apart a firm relationship can hardly be denied.

In respect to the Oakland Purchase incident the close friendship of William Heath Davis and James Alexander Forbes was made quite evident. Now, in later years, J. A. Forbes, Junior, was properly recognized as an excellent translator. Junior had been born at Santa Clara and was, of course, the nephew of Encarnación Galindo Peralta.

In 1865-67, the young man had been employed at the State Capitol to translate laws into Spanish for publication. His translation for the court a decade later in the Encinal case has already been noted. On November 22, 1881, when he wrote to "Dear Friend" William H. Davis, Forbes was a dissatisfied translator in the General Land Office earning 116 dollars monthly.

After informing Davis that he had done all he possibly could in some land case he asked for a favor in return. He desired preferably to be appointed American Consul at Guaymas or Mazatlan or else "the old man's place. . . . Here I am as you know translating twice as much as Clar in one day and he receives $2,000 a year."

Young Forbes went on to say, "Your influence and recommendation with such eminent gentlemen as the Hon. Mr. Page and my dear Friend Pacheco is no doubt invaluable and I rely on your good efforts to get what I ask."[34]

At this time California was represented in the House of Representatives by four Congressmen. The district of Horace F. Page

---

[34]W. Edwin Gledhill, Director of Santa Barbara Historical Museum simply happened upon the loose Forbes-Davis letter in a book on California history written by the third and eldest James Alexander Forbes (presumably no relative). Gledhill recognized the name Clar since he had been helping with local research but, of course, could not know how valuable his find was in developing this story.

included the pie-shaped wedge of gold country east of the Bay, from Nevada to Tuolumne counties, inclusive. Romualdo Pacheco represented northern California north of the Bay and Sacramento and Nevada counties. William S. Rosecrans, formerly of the Union Army and U. S. Minister to Mexico, represented populous San Francisco County. The other district included the entire southern and central portion of the State.

Pacheco in 1875 became the first native-born American Governor of California. He was born in Santa Barbara. And during the Clar's residence in that city he had been State Senator representing Santa Barbara and San Luis Obispo counties. The two men should have been longtime acquaintences. Clar and Rosecrans were certainly known to be friends, at least since the General had settled in San Francisco.[35]

On August 1st, 1882, William H. Brown, U. S. Surveyor-General for California, transmitted an elaborately printed form letter which declared, "Reposing special trust and confidence in the integrity, ability and discretion of John Clar, I hereby appoint and employ him . . . to serve in the capacity of *Translator* . . . "

Nevertheless, about a year later the effect of Forbes' efforts to push him out of his job must have caused Clar to feel that a supporting anchor in Washington might be a substantial aid riding out this last rough weather.

Probably Patrick J. Thomas, the father-in-law of son Maurice, suggested contacting Alex M. Kenady. Thomas was a well-known and probably politically influential publisher in San Francisco. And Kenady had also been in newspaper work after his arrival on the *Humboldt* in 1849. Now he was Secretary of the Association of Mexican War Veterans in Washington. The need, the timing, and especially the structure of Clar's letter of September 16, 1883, point strongly to the validity of these assumptions.

Kenady's sincere respect for John Clar is hardly to be questioned although whatever direct action he may have taken in response to the long letter of September 16, 1883, is not known. A few months later he published the greater part of the letter with his own warm tribute as an obituary and memorial for the writer.

The biographical features of the letter have already been used to good advantage. The veiled political aspects should also be

---

[35]The writer has an original note of philosophical comment penned for his Aunt Anne (wife of Maurice) by Congressman Wm. S. Rosecrans, about 1882. The memento had been preserved by her granddaughter Angèle Beatrice (Shaw).

mentioned. For example, Clar suggested that a word of commendation from such a well-known person as Kenady "might prove of service for my continuance in office in my present position if the case should be mooted. I have in case of need the good offices of the learned General Rosecrans and others."

In respect to the *Humboldt* brotherhood, he declared, "I have also received tokens of commendation from our friend Mr. Huntington which have rendered me signal service."

The most subtle name-dropping came in the listing of accomplishments, which were, of course, presented as his qualifications to remain in a modest government post. He wrote, "In 1832, though my senior in years, I gave lessons to the father-in-law of our President Mr. Arthur." The reference was to Midshipman William L. Herndon who was Clar's age. That experience had been a half-century and a world behind. Herndon, incidentally, was lost at sea with his vessel and entire command in 1857.

Clar's exasperation, as expressed in the following quotation from the letter, might well have been simmering during the 25 years since his discharge from the General Land Office in 1858. Not since his angry accusation directed toward the Secretary of the Navy in 1847 had this man cried out so vehemently at what he obviously considered a personal injustice. He declared,

> . . . for these 31 years I have been employed as a mathematician and Spanish translator in this U. S. Surveyor-General's office, barring some interruptions brought on by political tricksters. I know a little of almost everything except low politics. A crowd of numskulls have often applied for my place, and not strange to say they have sometimes succeeded, but somehow or other my head has invariably been put back on my shoulders.

The case of the old man's position apparently did not become a mooted question. He died quietly at the Polk Street residence on Sunday evening, April 27, 1884. Said the *Morning Call*, in keeping with other long biographical sketches in local papers, "Up to the day of his death he was employed in the office of the United States Surveyor-General. Everyone who knew Captain Clar knew him as a warm friend and genial companion."

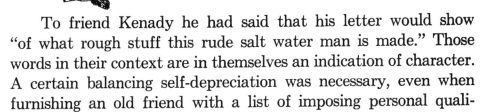

To friend Kenady he had said that his letter would show "of what rough stuff this rude salt water man is made." Those words in their context are in themselves an indication of character. A certain balancing self-depreciation was necessary, even when furnishing an old friend with a list of imposing personal qualifications to be recited in places of political power.

In the days of iron-fisted military discipline, petty officer Meyers had referred to his friend Professor Clar as a democratic officer.

To the whole external world, including his own family, he unquestionably presented himself as he truly thought of himself— a cultured Old World Cavalier. For example, rigid as were the social formalities of that Victorian Age, this man could not have been writing mere idle rhetoric in a very personal letter to his 25-year-old son. Upon learning of the latter's courteous reception of a new sister-in-law he wrote, "I knew you would, from the gallant stock from whence you come. Politeness to the ladies is a mark of refined education."

So he had lived hopefully and labored, contributing a few things of worth, and he died and was mourned by four stalwart sons and numerous friends.

A half century after his death, when the increasing congestion of a living city would no longer tolerate the few quiet acres set aside for the unprotesting and generally forgotten dead, the remains of John and Angèle Clar were removed to the National Cemetery at San Francisco Presidio. A granite block there marks their names and dates and indicates that John was a Professor of Mathematics in the Navy.

Mr. Iron Clar,

San Francisco March 15th 1863
Thursday evening

God bless my dear son Iron

Do you know you have written to me a letter
which afforded me great pleasure? It is plain but most
sincere and penned with so natural a style that every
word of it went to the core of my heart. I am glad
you are pleased with the situation, but you know not
how much I miss your company. It is true that man
must earn his bread by labor, yet I would have been
better satisfied if you could have worked near me,
as it is, come down as often as you can.
In your pleasures be always moderate, for this is the
science of true enjoyment, but I need say no more on
that score. You are prudent and judicious and I
know you will without effort practice the four cardinal
virtues and these are: Justice, temperance, prudence
and fortitude. Therein lies true morality. I would
have you also peruse the Commandments – they suit
all ages and conditions of men. Do not neglect the
New testament, for it contains all the lessons of religion
and morality, particularly the Sermon on the mount
which is the best Sermon ever preached in this world.
The rich, the poor, the healthy, the sickly all can learn of good

lesson therefrom

When you get your Cornet I know you will I know you will make the hills and the dales reverberate Melodious sounds, but an excess of blowing might be hurtful to the lungs – so be moderate in that as in every thing you do.

Should you meet with any Contrariety, do not hesitate, but come down to us.

The Mine they say is very rich, but I fear they work it too slowly. The old Cook is ever growling but she wishes she Could give you some of her good things, thinking you get but mighty few delicacies she often speaks of you. I would go up to see you but I am so dilapidated and delicate that it would no doubt hurt me.

I wish in many things you Could imitate your good brother Lawrence, I almost think him perfection, but for that severe ascetic manner of his Composition, Leo is mightily attached to you. He wants to insert a note herein That God may bless and protect you and the other brothers is the sincere prayer of your most affectionate

John Clar

Letter of John Clar to his 25-year-old bachelor son about eleven months before the old man's death. The son was then engaged in redwood lumbering on the Russian River. The letter's formal style was undoubtedly very proper at the time. Yet a great personal warmth and sincerity are quite evident. It is possible that the aged father, perhaps even subconsciously, considered this to be his last bequest to all of his sons. He had no material possessions to assign and bequeath. From one who had seen so much of the world, what better legacy than this admonition to adhere always to the principles of justice, temperance, prudence and fortitude? A later letter referred to the gold mine as probably a wildcat speculation. Probably this was John Clar's only direct association with gold mining.

*At the foot of the slope below the cemetery,*
  *and below the remnants of the old Spanish Fort*
  *the eternal tides ebb and flow through the Golden Gate.*
*And beyond the Monterey cypress*
  *surrounding the hallowed ground*
  *great bridge pillars and the bare Marin hills*
  *stand against the northern sky.*
*Only when turbulent outer seas smash the rocky toes of Lands End*
  *can the rumble of wild surf be heard*
  *above the continuous murmur of motor traffic.*
*And on a summer afternoon, when vanguard ghosts of incoming fog*
  *slide around the massive towers,*
  *anyone who wills it can surely see,*
  *among the drifting fog wisps,*
  *the white and silent sails of the argonaut ships*
  *coming to rest at the end of their journey.*

## CHRONOLOGY OF THE LIFE OF JOHN CLAR

May 1813:       born at Port Mahon, Menorca, Spain.

circa 1820:     begins sailor's career on the Mediterranean.

May 1831:       graduated from Spanish Naval Academy.

Dec. 1832:      signed aboard U.S. Frigate *Constellation* as School Master.

Dec. 1834:      arrives U.S., probably Philadelphia.

May 1835:       aboard Sloop of War *Peacock* as School Master and Commodore's private clerk, sailing eastward around world.

Sept. 1835:     aground off Mazeira, Arabia.

Oct. 1836:      visits Monte-Rey, Alta California.

Oct. 1837:      arrives "home" Norfolk, Virginia.

May 1838:       aboard Frigate *Columbia*, again eastward around world.

Jan. 1839:      bombardment of pirates at Meuké.

June 1840:      arrives Hampton Roads, Virginia; assigned shore classes at Philadelphia.

Oct. 1841:      Commissioned Professor of Mathematics and assigned to Sloop of War *Cyane*.

Nov. 1841:      *Cyane* leaves Norfolk for Pacific Naval Station.

Oct. 1842:      Monterey captured by Commodore Thomas ap Catesby Jones; Clar is interpreter of landing party and Secretary of State in Military Government.

Dec. 1842:      he first views Yerba Buena Village.

May 1843:       sent to Sonoma to arrest Salvador Vallejo.

Fall 1843:      about Sandwich Islands.

Dec. 1843:      at San Francisco Bay again.

June 1844:      transferred to Frigate *Savannah*.

Summer 1844:    about the Sandwich Islands.

March 1845:     Callao, Peru; medical examination and transfer to United States on sick leave by order of Commodore Sloat.

July 1845:      arrives Boston on merchant ship *Robin Hood;* reports illness to Navy Secretary Bancroft.

1845:           professorship of French at new Annapolis Academy declined because of his illness.

Aug. 1846:      annual sickness pension of $240 is granted.

Spring 1847:    request for active duty refused, pension terminated.

Sept. 1847:     resigns from Navy in anger.

1848:           railroad construction engineering in Vermont and Massachusetts.

| | |
|---|---|
| April 1849: | at Panama via the Isthmus route. Becomes sailing master of barque *Alex von Humboldt*. |
| Sept. 1849: | arrives in San Francisco after difficult voyage. Offered command of *Humboldt*. |
| Sept. 1851: | elected Surveyor of Marin County; |
| Oct. 1851: | contracts to purchase present downtown Oakland from Peralta. |
| Dec. 1851: | hired as technical clerk by Land Claims Commission. |
| March 1852: | sale transaction of Oakland to Clar, et al. |
| Aug. 1852: | resigns from Land Claims Commission. |
| Oct. 1852: | hired by U. S. Land Office as Keeper of Old Archives and Translator. |
| Oct. 1853: | married by Archbishop Alemany in San Francisco to Angèle Beatrice Lesgent of Paris. |
| Oct. 1855: | formally naturalized a U.S. Citizen. |
| Spring 1857: | takes up land claim at Geyserville-Clarville. |
| Oct. 1857: | separated from Land Office |
| Jan. 1859: | sells the Clar Ranch. |
| March 1859: | applies for State translator job. |
| 1859: | family moves to Santa Barbara. |
| Nov. 1860: | elected County Superintendent of Schools. |
| May 1861: | appointed Justice of Peace in Santa Barbara. |
| 1863: | returns to San Francisco; Archivist and Translator in General Land Office. |
| 1868: | dismissed from Land Office. |
| Oct. 1868: | surveyor for State Tidelands Commission and private jobs. |
| 1879: | rehired by Land Office as Translator and Keeper of Old Archives. |
| April 1880: | Madame Clar dies at store-home, 1220 Polk Street. |
| April 1884: | John Clar dies at same residence. |
| 1930: | remains removed to S. F. Presidio National Cemetery. |

# Acknowledgment

It is not conceivable that a book of this nature could be written without the generous assistance of many persons and institutions. The author deeply appreciates the assistance he has received throughout this Nation and in Spain. Some contributors are mentioned in the text or notes, wherever it was deemed worth while to identify sources for the benefit of later scholars. And at the serious risk of failing to remember some of the worthy names, the author must list here a few to whom he is indebted.

Among *librarians* there were Evelyn Huston of U. of C. Irvine, Richard Dillon at Sutro, Albert Harmon at the S. F. Maritime Museum; Director James D. Hart, Robert Becker and John B. Tompkins of Bancroft; Helen S. Giffen of the Society of California Pioneers; Arthur Kirby at Norfolk, Virginia; Frances H. Buxton of Oakland, Dorothy Thomas of Mill Valley, Peter Evans of the California Historical Society, and especially Allan R. Ottley and his staff at the California State Library.

Among *archivists and recorders* there were the Clerks of the California Supreme Court and the U. S. Admiralty Court; the County Recorders of San Francisco, Alameda, Contra Costa, Marin, Sonoma and Santa Barbara. For ecclesiastical records the author is indebted to the Reverend Maynard Geiger and Father Henry Busch at Santa Barbara and Father Fernando Martí at Mahón, Spain. There were W. Edwin Gledhill, Director of Santa Barbara Historical Museum, Dr. J. N. Bowman, and David Snyder of State Archives. As critic, contributor and historical analyst, Dr. William N. Davis, Jr., Chief of State Archives, was continuously helpful.

In Washington several branches of the National Archives responded with valuable information. The author thanks Miss Jane Smith and Richard S. Maxwell of Social and Economic Records; Mark G. Eckhoff of Diplomatic, Legal, and Fiscal Records; Elbert L. Huber of the Navy Branch of War Records; Admiral E. M. Eller, Director of Naval History; and G. E. Hasselwander of the Interior Branch of Natural Resources Archives. Henry Clepper of Washington made special searches at the author's urgent request.

A number of individuals contributed in various ways. Harold L. Johnson suggested the title and read the manuscript, as did Esther Gall and Beverly Peterson. John C. Schubert at Santa Rosa and

Lucretia Little at Mill Valley searched old county records. In the Division of State Lands, Robert G. Nadey and John Snell discovered interesting survey records. Raymond Tatian, Dorthy McGill and Ruth Hunter, literally applied their hands to the project. Enrique and Elizabeth Edwards of Sacramento interpreted the Royal Naval Academy Certificate and personally carried their investigation into the *Museo Naval* at Madrid. Not least to be remembered are those other descendants of John and Angèle who helped where they could, my sister, brothers and cousins, and "Aunt Belle" Clar of San Francisco, who was surprised that so much could be written about her late husband's parents.

Sacramento, 1970

---

### The Author

Charles Raymond Clar is the third son of John Clar's second son. The author was born in Guerneville, Sonoma County, a couple of years after the mills had finished sawing the last great virgin redwood trees of that vicinity. He attended Santa Rosa High School by commuting 22 miles each school day on the steam train. In 1927 he was graduated from the University of California with a degree in forestry.

For 42 years, until his retirement in 1969, he was employed by the California State Division of Forestry. He had the opportunity to play a considerable part in the development of that organization as he rose to a responsible administrative position. Much of the author's official career is reflected in his two volume history published by the State and titled *California Government and Forestry*. For that accomplishment and for the production of numerous technical writings of similar nature, the author was elected a Fellow of the Forest History Society. He is also a member of the California Writers Club and the Society of California Pioneers.

# BIBLIOGRAPHY

Newspapers and other specific reference sources are footnoted throughout the text.

## MANUSCRIPT AND NEWSPAPERS

Personal letters, memoranda and notebooks of John Clar.

Official documents and letters in government archives and historical depositories.

*"Journal of a Cruise to California . . ."* by Wm. H. Meyers (1839-43).

Lands Claims Commission files, and court records.

Current newspaper sources, principally the S. F. *Alta California* and *Daily Herald* and the *Panama Star.*

## GENERAL HISTORY

*History of California,* vols. 2-5, by H. H. Bancroft (S.F., 1886)

*History of California,* vol. 2 by T. H. Hittell, (S.F., 1885)

*California Pastoral,* H. H. Bancroft (1886)

*California from the Conquest in 1846 to the Second Vigilante Committee in S.F.,* by Josiah Royce (Boston, 1886)

*California Place Names,* Gudde, Edwin G. (U. of C. Press)

*Historic Spots in California,* Hoover and Rensch (Stanford U. Press, 1966)

## SHIPS

*The History of American Sailing Ships* by H. I. Chapelle (N.Y. 1935)

*A Voyage Around the World,* by W.S.W. Ruschenberger (Phila., 1838)

*Voyage Around the World,* by Fitch W. Taylor (N. Y. 1842)

*Wandering Sketches of People and Things,* by William Maxwell Wood (Phila., 1849)

*Thence Round Cape Horn* by Robert Erwin Johnson (U.S.N. Institute, 1963)

*California Diary of Foxen Dean Atherton* 1836-1839, ed. by Doyce B. Nunis, Cal. Hist. Soc., (1964)

*Cal. Historical Society Quarterly,*
"Commodore Edmund B. Kennedy, U.S.N., Versus Governor Nicolas Gutierrez, An Incident of 1836," by George Tays, June 1933

*The Pioneer,* Soc. Cal. Pioneers, 1944,
*"Voyage of the Old Ship Humboldt"* by James Gordon.

## LANDS AND POLITICS

*Hutching's California Magazine*
"Mexican Land Claims in California" by John S. Hittell, April 1858

*History of Bench and Bar,* by Oscar T. Shucks (S.F. 1900)

*Cal. Hist. Society Quarterly*
"Rise and fall of the Know Nothing Party," by Peyton Hurt, March 1930

"Santa Barbara County Between Two Social Orders," by Walter C. McKain, Dec 1946

"Evolution of Weights and Measures in New Spain" by J. N. Bowman, Dec 1951

*Decline of the Californios,* by Leonard Pitt (U. C. Press, 1966)

*Letters of John Q. Adams Warren, "Cal. Ranchos and Farms, 1846-1862"* by Paul Gates (State Hist. Soc. of Wisconsin, 1967)

*Sixty Years in California,* by William Heath Davis (S.F. 1889)

*The Centennial Yearbook of Alameda County* by William Halley (1876)

*Past and Present of Alameda County,* by Joseph E. Baker (1914)

*Colonel Jack Hays,* by James K. Greer (N.Y. 1952)

*Cal. Hist. Soc. Quarterly*

"Julias Kellersberger: A Swiss Surveyor and City Planner in California" by Jack J. Studer, March 1968

"The First Map of Oakland, California: An Historical Speculation as Solution to an Enigma," by Jack J. Studer, March 1969

*History of Marin County,* Alley Bowen Co. (S.F. 1880)

*History of Sonoma County,* Alley Bowen Co. (S.F. 1880)

*The Vallejos of California,* by Madie Brown Emparan (1968 Univ. of S.F.)

*Mountains and Molehills,* by Francis S. Marryat (N.Y. 1855)

*Life and Adventures of Colonel L. A. Norton,* by L. A. Norton, (Oakland 1887)

*A History of the Bowers Map Bill,* by A. B. Bowers (Eastman Pub. S.F. 1869)

### STATE DOCUMENTS

*Journals* of the Calif. Senate and Assembly

*Reports* of the State Surveyor-General

# Index

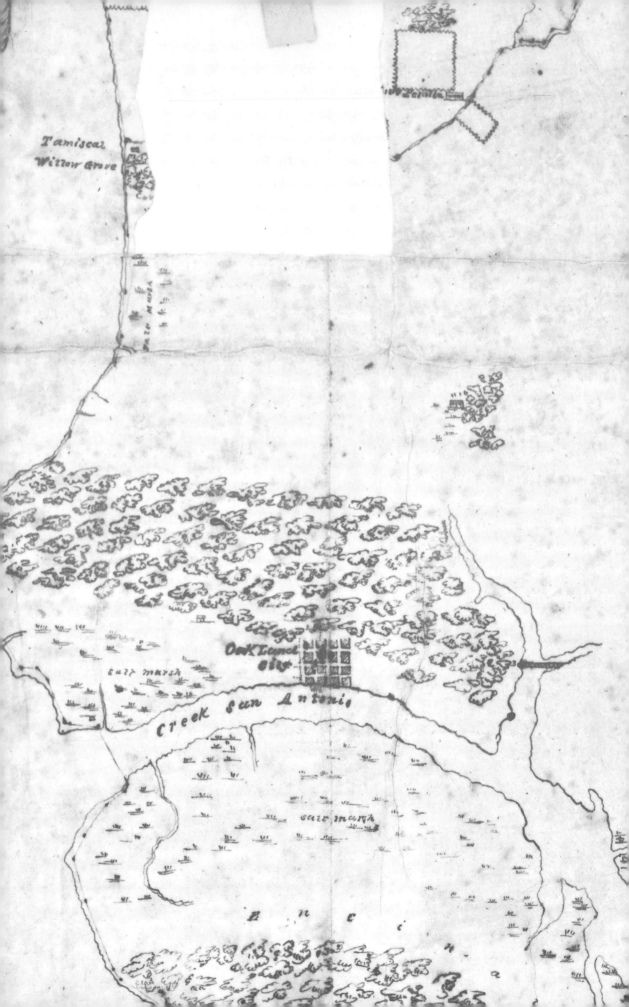

Tamiscal
Willow Grove

Salt marsh

Oakland City

salt marsh

Creek San Antonio

salt marsh

R a n c i